M000314555

# Praise for Ricci-Jane and
## *Spiritually Fierce*

"I believe that Ricci-Jane Adams is at the top of her profession, and her book commands our respect both for its fine-tuned guidance and told in a most entertaining fashion. I have read Spiritually Fierce twice and have recommended it to many as I believe that Ricci-Jane's book is arguably one of the finest in its field. I only wish I were in the area so I could attend one of Adam's seminars... With my whole heart, I recommend that you buy it, read it, recommend it, and rejoice in the difference it will make in your life." Jean Sasson, New York Times Bestseller, author of the Princess book series

"This is not a one-time read. *Spiritually Fierce* by Dr Ricci-Jane Adams is now one of my all-time fave books that I will read time and again, to help me connect into the word of the universe, to tune into my oneness, it's the Gabby Bernstein and Wayne Dyer and Eckhart Tolle I crave, all rolled into one.

This book came to me at just the right time – amid a personal challenge. These times always call for a renewed focus on how we understand ourselves and how we can grow through the struggle. Ricci-Jane builds on my knowledge of how we can be and shows me how to practice and delve into my Intuitive Intelligence on a daily basis, how to return to it, how to remind myself to come from that heart space and to be in love." Sarah Nimarota

"This book is a must-read for every person on the planet! Spiritually Fierce is THE tool to empower a new generation of love warriors. It explains the concepts, ideas and 'how to' to access and cultivate your own spiritual self-esteem, Intuitive Intelligence and wisdom of the heart to live a life of joy, bliss and love. It is fantastically articulated and presents complex ideas in an easy to understand way. Thank you, Ricci-Jane Adams- for presenting this work to the world, so we can ALL find and utilise the divine perfection that is within us!! Come get spiritually fierce with us- you won't regret it!" Bek Tomarchio

"A must-read for those on the spiritual path. Dr Ricci-Jane Adams has such a beautiful way of sharing her own journey and wisdom from her own experiences but also making the information and practices accessible, easy, and joyful. A true guiding light for seekers." Karen Buckland

"*Spiritually Fierce* by Dr Ricci-Jane Adams, beautifully blends her own personal stories with the science of intuition, to educate and inspire both men and women worldwide to not only embrace their intuition but on how to implement and live with Intuitive Intelligence on a daily basis.

Her book not only covers an in-depth background on the theories and scientific research of intuition but offers effective, practical tips and tools for the reader on how to recognise, grow and utilise their own intuition to live from the heart space, in a more connected and spiritually fierce life.

This is a book that gifts real ah-ha moments, epiphanies around our own fears and beliefs and most importantly, it is a book that allows for healing of the separateness within ourselves. By this, I don't just mean physical healing but healing of our thoughts, our mental state and the beliefs we hold about ourselves and the world we live in. Dr Ricci-Jane Adams has much to teach those searching for that something more, that state of higher consciousness, of knowing and trusting that each and every one of us are part of the divine and infinite. It's a call to return home.

In truth, *Spiritually Fierce* is not just a book; it's an effective and resourceful guidebook for anyone who wants to understand, nurture, and embrace their Intuitive Intelligence; not as a current trend but with a fierce commitment to their own beautiful personal and spiritual growth and development.

It's a book I'll be keeping close at hand for continuous reflection and reference to remind me of who I really am, and the power within." Verity Nimmo Mansfield

"It is hard to believe that *Spiritually Fierce* is a debut piece. This may have something to do with the fact that Dr Ricci-Jane Adams is writing her life in these pages. Through Spiritually Fierce she shares her journey to discovering her true path as well as all she has learned through over 20 years of study into the science of intuition and the human energy field.

This book is perfect for both the beginner spiritual seeker as well as those who are a little more advanced on the journey. It brings together practical examples from Adams' personal and professional experiences along with the great spiritual teachings of masters such as Caroline Myss, Marianne Williamson and Gregg Braden. Real-life examples are woven in with scientifically proven techniques to help readers raise their vibration and start living their best possible life.

When she is not authoring spiritual texts, Ricci-Jane Adams is Director of the Institute of Intuitive Intelligence, where she teaches her students - you guessed it - how to get spiritually fierce.

Ricci-Jane's writing style is conversational enough to be an easy read while at the same time packed with evidence to substantiate every single claim she makes about the science of intuition (did I mention she's also an academic?!)

In this book, Ricci-Jane shares the tools she has used to align her day-to-day life with her bliss. Read this book, treasure it, memorise the tools within and perhaps you too can bring the life you dream of into being?!

This might be the first offering from Ricci-Jane Adams, but it definitely won't be the last. Get into it now so you can say you knew her before she became a household name." Jo McEniery

Dr Ricci-Jane Adams is the principal of the Institute for Intuitive Intelligence®, a world-class, professional intuition training school. She trains exceptional spiritual people in the science and mysticism of Intuitive Intelligence®. The Institute leads the way in academic rigour, ethical grounding and social conscience, bringing a gold standard of professional excellence to an unregulated industry. Ricci-Jane is the author of bestselling *Spiritually Fierce*, as well as *Intuitive Intelligence Training*. Ricci-Jane has a doctorate from the University of Melbourne in magical realism. She has spent over twenty-five years devoted to her spiritual awakening and is a qualified Transpersonal Counsellor.

First published by Institute for Intuitive Intelligence in 2022
https://instituteforintuitiveintelligence.com/

Copyright © Ricci-Jane Adams 2022
http://www.riccijaneadams.com/

All quotes from *A Course in Miracles*© are from thttps://acim.org/acim/en, by
the Foundation for Inner Peace, P.O. Box 598, Mill Valley, CA 94942-
0598, www.acim.org and info@acim.org.

Superconscious Intuition

Ebook format: 9780648095057
Print: 9780648095064

Cover and interior design by Elise Elliott hello@passthesalt.com.au
All interior images by Rachael Cannard ours@notminenotyours.com
Cover photo and author image by Zaharoula Harris
info@corporateheadshotsmelbourne.com.au

# Superconscious Intuition

## Intuition beyond the trinkets and superstitions of the new age

Ricci-Jane Adams 2022

This one is for my boys, Finn and Luka, who make everything glorious just by being in the world.

# Foreword

For more than 40 years, I have been captivated by the promise of a mystical aspect to my life. I sought a mystical experience that would colour and inspire my otherwise ordinary existence. I was looking for an escape from the world that didn't reflect my magical truth.

My pilgrimage down this yellow brick road was diverse and often took me to places and people that offered great adventures and much travel. But I was always an observer, rarely ever in that place of inspiration. No matter how many spiritual modalities I learned and taught, I could not find the essence of myself.

I was making the same fundamental error that many of my fellow seekers were making. I was always looking out there and looking to others for their magic to inspire my magic. It doesn't seem to happen that way.

Eventually, I learned that it is an inward journey to uncover these universal aspects that resonate with All that Is. Everything is energy at every level of our being. Our task is learning that our energy can be impacted, redesigned and reinvented by us!

In so doing, we learn our lives are all about the greatest gift, *freedom of choice*. With this gift, we can recognise our ability to be the designer and the architect, rebuilding and rejuvenating every aspect of ourselves. We do this just by making another choice, a more healing choice, in this moment. We are heading towards our mystical, magical truth as we do this — the knowledge that *we* are love. *Unconditional love.* Our journey of freedom of choice is all we need to uncover and eliminate the belief systems that hold us from the experience of knowing ourselves as unconditional love, peacefulness and joy.

Dr Ricci-Jane Adams journeys to greater heights in her exciting new book, *Superconscious Intuition.* Encouraging us beyond the limits we have imposed on ourselves and inviting us to awaken from the dream. As Ricci-Jane puts it, to 'activate our highest form of intuition to facilitate the awakening to the truth of what we are'.

This book is not for the faint of heart. It is a vigorous examination of the human experiment on Planet Earth. The exciting thing around this level of our knowledge of ourselves as spiritual and human beings, with all our levels of complexity, is that scientific research is now climbing the mountain and showing us how very capable we can become.

As we learn to challenge the inter-generational beliefs we were born into, the limitations of our society and our safe place within it, we begin to find new levels of freedom. We found the freedom to expand our thoughts about ourselves and to be able to recognise how much power we have invested in supporting the fears that enslave us.

Ricci-Jane is the creator and director of The Institute for Intuitive Intelligence. Within the Institute, she offers a variety of programs designed to support exceptional spiritual people as they challenge their limitations and access superconsciousness. *Superconscious Intuition* clearly defines the potential within us all. This book (and the attendant program) supports us as we journey toward the Eternal Light of our freedom. It is a gift that many of my generation would have felt blessed to discover.

And speaking of generations, Dr Ricci-Jane Adams is my daughter. It is exciting to see my early work in self-discovery flying high through her efforts. Know that this, her latest book, is a strong read. It is not something to pick up and read as you drop off to sleep. It demands attention, and your effort will be rewarded.

Some of the ideas presented may challenge your comfort zones. Sit with them anyway. Allow the possibility they offer before deciding they are not a fit for you. Remember, you are being invited to glimpse your potential beyond your beliefs of what defines you. Welcome to your superconsciousness.

Angelique Adams
March 2022

# Contents

Preface ............................................................................................. 1

Introduction: The Beginning Of Intuition Is The End Of Intuition .............. 6

**Part One: Foundations** ................................................................... 23

Chapter 1: The Laws Of Superconsciousness ................................... 25

Chapter 2: The Science Of Superconsciousness .......................... 40

Chapter 3: The Layers Of Consciousness .................................... 49

Chapter 4: The Function Of Fear .................................................. 58

**Part Two: The Evolution** ................................................................ 81

Chapter 5: The Phases Of Intuition Maturity ................................. 83

Chapter 6: Our Biology Is The Technology Of Our Intuition .................. 122

Chapter 7: What Is A Trinket And Superstition Of The New Age? .......... 137

**Part Three: The Revolution** .......................................................... 165

Chapter 8: Creating Space .......................................................... 167

Chapter 9: If You Think You Need Protection... ........................... 177

Chapter 10: Rebellious Acceptance And Radical Advantageousness ....... 190

Chapter 11: Superconscious Gloriousness ................................... 202

Conclusion: Meeting Ourselves As Superconscious Leaders .................... 216

Acknowledgements ..................................................................... 222

About Dr Ricci-Jane Adams .......................................................... 224

About Superconscious Intuition The Program ............................ 227

"You are at home in God, dreaming of exile but perfectly capable of awakening to reality."

—A Course In Miracles

# Preface

## I left my husband for God

*"Tell me, what is it you plan to do*
*with your one wild and precious life?"*

— *Mary Oliver*

January 6 2020, was not a typical day for most Australians. Much of the east coast of Australia, where I live, was engulfed by massive bushfires unlike anything in living memory. In my suburb in the middle of Melbourne, my own home, far from the fires, was blanketed by smoke. The reality was everywhere and unavoidable.

Inside my home, another situation was also glaringly unavoidable. My husband and I sat across from each other in the living room. I think I was holding my breath as he asked,

*So are you done?*

The words rushed from me as though an invisible hand were thumping me on the back,

*Yes. I think it's time to end our marriage.*

I had held this thought in for so long. Too long. My husband looked at me from across the living room. We were both so tired. He replied gently,

1

*Me too.*

It was the miracle I had prayed for every day for months but hardly dared believe would be possible. To this day, we have managed one of the most amicable and open-hearted relationship endings that I have ever heard. But I should have known it would be this way. I knew this decision to end my marriage was a direct instruction from God.

For more than a year, our relationship hadn't been good. We both felt like our marriage did not meet our needs, and resentment was building. The Institute's rapid growth meant that I was travelling more and more, and my absence was a heavy burden for my husband. It hurt me that my success was a source of resentment. The truth was we wanted different things now. We had had an incredible 12 years, but it was time to let go.

*Let go,*

had been the constant guidance moving through me for months.

*It is safe to make this bold leap into the unknown. It is time for the next phase of your evolution.*

'*It*' felt so profoundly held. I knew it was direct instruction from my superconscious intuition and that everything would unfold with ease and grace, even if there were hard times. And there have been.

It felt, and still feels, like a spiritual calling. Instead of being called to take holy vows or walk the Camino, I was being asked in no uncertain terms to leave the comfort zone of domestic life behind and to align even more fiercely with my purpose. It was time for me to centre my relationship with God.

I remember something Sally Thurley said to me when I interviewed her a few years ago. It struck me so profoundly. *The mystical woman is the ultimate wild woman.* Taking God as my primary partner might seem reckless, but the wild intuitive knowing in me says otherwise. I have seen what happens when I choose my divine truth first and the consequences when I don't.

To choose to take God as my primary partner is to say that I choose myself above all else. It's a bold move. And an easy one to forget. To place our holiness first in a world obsessed with the external and material is an unpopular choice. But I am not the first to make it, and many have done so more boldly than by simply ending a relationship.

I also made that choice many times within my marriage, and without question, it contributed to the relationship's demise. I don't regret that. I had to become congruent with what God was asking of me (aka what I was asking of myself). The marriage wasn't the problem (although it was timely that we moved on). The problem was that I was clinging to my comfort zone by staying. For all the challenges between my husband and me, it was otherwise a very nice, very stable life that allowed me to focus on my mission without too much distraction.

I knew that when I listened to that voice within me, which was a roar by the time I finally spoke up, there would be an inevitable period of chaos and *loss of control*. I wouldn't be able to control my soon to be ex-husband's response. I wouldn't be able to control my childrens' responses. There would be uncertainty for everyone, emotionally, physically, and financially. Life would be in flux. And I was resisting it because I wanted to stay 100% focused on my mission.

But I could feel the more profound truth. **My mission, my work, my purpose are all the same thing. To know myself as God.** That shows up in the world through the work of the Institute and getting to support others also to know that they are God (because there is only one of us here, right?). My service is my medicine. And in staying in my comfort zone, no matter why, when God was calling me into bold action, was to betray my own divine, glorious nature.

Choosing God first isn't a choice I will only need to make once. It isn't an easy choice. But, for me, the only option is to privilege that wild, untamed wisdom within. In truth, I have made those bold, wild leaps in faith all my life. But as I got older and life felt more serious, the responsibilities more significant, including to two young men I am lucky enough to mother, I felt myself teetering on that precipice for longer and longer.

What is a well-lived life? For me, that answer is simple. To make choices in every moment that take me closer to remembering the truth that I AM God—through joy, pleasure, moonlight, heartache, doing the dishes, raising boys, eating, dancing, sobbing, grieving, in sucking the marrow from every moment. My life is so far out of my comfort zone you wouldn't believe it. But I cannot go wrong when my superconscious intuition leads the dance.

In case you too are feeling that ultimate of wild calls — to partner with your divinity and leave the world of the known behind, then you are so welcome here. Being in our divinity, paradoxically, makes us more empowered to participate in the world. As divine beings in a human experience, we can honestly know the world, not fade away in the illusion of the comfort zone.

I have learnt to privilege the voice of the deepest state of intuition — superconscious intuition — over decades of practice and learning and humbly failing again and again. It is a lifelong love affair to become intimate with the voice of my soul and to lead my life from that place. I invite you to join me to do the same.

# Introduction

# The Beginning of Intuition is the end of Intuition

*"The superconscious mind is the God Mind within each man, and is the realm of perfect ideas."*
— *Florence Scovel Shinn*

Intuition is the gateway to opening to our divine nature for so many of us. We have enough synchronicity experiences or knowing that we follow that divine lead without knowing how we know. We enrol in a tarot class, sign up for a psychic development workshop or join a mediumship circle. This is, or at least it should be, the beginning of changing our perception of reality and ourselves. But it so rarely is. More often than not, it creates more separation thinking and barely improves the lives of those who access intuition at this level except in the most superficial ways.

My last book, *Spiritually Fierce,* was all about intuition and how to increase it by learning to trust it and live it. It was a timely book, the first place that intuition development and the immutable laws are synergised. It opened and continues to open many people to the deeper power and truth of their intuition beyond the trinkets and superstitions of the new age. Now I am ready to go further and share an even more fierce and uncompromising discussion of the true nature of our spiritual superpower.

In this book, my contention is this.

*There is no such thing as intuition.* We are all in temporary amnesia that we will wake up from collectively. As we do, conversations about intuition, what it is, where it resides in the body, how to access it will all become redundant.

When we have remembered what we are, why would we need a language to communicate with ourselves? Why would we need a bridge between us and ourselves? We will simply no longer require this construct called intuition.

Intuition is a function of consciousness. As we increase our connection to our intuition, we raise our consciousness and vice versa.

If science were ever to figure out how consciousness truly functions, it would be like pulling out the plug from the wall of the Universe, and we would all just disappear. If we solve that mystery, the need for our existence comes to an end. The pursuit of what we are and how and why we function is the work of our lives.

The endpoint of figuring out our consciousness is knowing that we are God. When we use the word, God, what we are trying to do, awkwardly, because there truly is nothing in the language that captures it effectively enough, is to reach the state of *unlimited consciousness*, which I refer to as superconsciousness.

The path of deep intuition, superconscious intuition, is uncompromising because it will ask us to put down all perceived limitations and go directly towards that truth that we are God.

What does that mean? It means that we are that which created consciousness. Consciousness is a function of our awakening. It is a tool we can utilise to manufacture a reality that wakes us up to the truth that we are God. Intuition is consciousness in communication. Superconscious intuition is the highest, most pure expression of our intuition. When we realise our superconsciousness, we are on the precipice of having no more need for intuition as we have understood it for so long.

Perhaps we didn't know when we picked up our first set of oracle cards that this is where that gateway drug would lead us, but it is an inevitable journey for all of us. 'You are at home in God, dreaming of exile but perfectly capable of awakening to reality.'[1] So says *A Course in Miracles*, and this statement brings me back to the truth faster than anything else.

I will not ask us to believe more about intuition. I am going to ask us to believe less. Much less. So much of the teachings of intuition in the world right now delay our awakening rather than encourage it. We become enamoured with the trinkets and superstitions. We look to be soothed in our littleness rather than inspired by our gloriousness. Think about it. When was it you last reached for an oracle deck or booked in with a psychic? Most likely, it was when you needed soothing. Life was feeling overwhelming, perhaps, or you were at a crossroads. You wanted something or someone else to carry the burden of your life for a little while, as though something out there knew the 'right answer' and could do the work for you.

---

1 *A Course in Miracles*, | T-10.I.2:1. Accessed at: https://acim.org/acim/en/s/139#2:1

That's how it was for me recently. I was in my home city of Melbourne during the first year of the Covid-19 Pandemic. We experienced the strictest and most prolonged lockdown of any place in the world at that time. My marriage had ended, and I was navigating that amongst a severe lockdown. I was homeschooling my children, unable to leave my house for more than an hour each day, and restricted within a five-kilometre radius when we did get to step outdoors. At the same time, the Institute was experiencing a rapid period of growth, and I was busier than ever. It was an unprecedented time, and I recall so vividly feeling this deep desire to no longer have to hold it all together, to be able to pass on some of this feeling of responsibility.

I reached out to Luh Manis, the Balinese Priestess I am lucky enough to consider my friend, and asked her to arrange a palm reading with her teacher. A week later, I was on a Zoom call with Luh from her home in Ubud as she shared with me what her teacher had divined from the image of my palm. Putu is a very profound channel for divine grace. But suffice to say, nothing she shared I didn't already know. As Luh continued to share the reading with me, I could feel her spiritual fierceness growing. Eventually, she said, almost exasperated,

*Ricci, this time is for all spiritual teachers to show up more and give more. We must increase our devotion now. The world demands this of us at this extraordinary time.*

I looked at that glorious woman through the computer screen, and I could have kissed her. Here was the guidance I needed. There was no mysterious future outcome that I could hear about that would alleviate my feelings of burden. Luh was so lovingly reminding me that this was my holy task to lead this revolution and go towards what I was afraid of. So I took her advice to heart and doubled down on my devotion. It was, after all, the most potent way for me to be of service to myself and all human consciousness.

Intuition and the development of our intuition reflect the development of our consciousness. Intuition is a spiritual faculty, not a new-age trinket. The more we refine our consciousness through our devotion and commitment to know ourselves as God, our intuition has more potency. Intuition is a tool, not the result. It is a byproduct of our awakening. And the endpoint, the future of our individual and collective intuition, the revolution, is that we will evolve beyond the need for it.

## How this book works

*Superconscious Intuition* is a collection of essays on the theory and praxis of Intuitive Intelligence. It has developed over five years of serving the Institute for Intuitive Intelligence's students across all our programs worldwide.

The ideas, theories, contentions and secondary analysis presented in this book have mostly been shared in live training and presentations first and then transcribed and edited to communicate in written form. My most effortless form of expression is verbal, so this text has a conversational tone. I have chosen to conserve this rather than to edit it away so that we may have a sense of sitting in the same space as each other!

I have also chosen to conserve the oral /aural sense in writing to honour the students, audiences and different groups who have inspired the words. These ideas don't happen in isolation. They are the result of the alchemy of the speaker and listener, the student and the teacher. The nature of my work is, unsurprisingly, intuitive, and so often, the words I share fall from me from that superconsciousness of which we are all a part. If one student, or one person in the Zoom room, or the audience had been different, would these exact words in this same order have emerged?

In other words, this text is a testament to learning by doing. Through living, sharing and exploring Intuitive Intelligence in my service as the principal of the Institute, this work has emerged. These words have been spoken out loud worldwide from Italy to Ireland to Australia and reached ears in Luxembourg, Colombia, New Zealand and everywhere in between. They represent the work of the Institute from 2017 to 2021.

The ideas pick up where my first book, *Spiritually Fierce,* left off and, in some ways, may contradict some of the teachings of that book. For the readers of the first book, I approach these new ideas with curiosity. We will gather enough evidence in these pages to see a different paradigm of possibility about ourselves and intuition. This evidence will point us toward the truth that we are superconscious. This is our birthright, and it is the precursor to us knowing ourselves as God, which is the endpoint of intuition. I have come to realise that my work resides at this *endpoint.*

I will never stop being a humble student of my intuition, so I do not doubt that my ideas will continue to evolve as my capabilities grow. I have also continued with what I began in *Spiritually Fierce* in mapping the work onto my life, or perhaps more accurately, mapping my life onto the work. Frequently these turning points weren't comfortable or desired, but I am not here in this life for my comfort. I am here for evolution — all of ours. I am not afraid to sweat for God. After all, when we live from our highest form of intelligence, our Intuitive

Intelligence, we are no longer experiencing the world through the human experience alone. We have become superconscious in our understanding of the world. And that's when life starts to get good.

The book is presented in three parts — the foundations for deep intuition, the evolution of Intuitive Intelligence, and the revolution of superconsciousness. There have been five years of research, teaching, and learning since writing *Spiritually Fierce*. Whilst *Spiritually Fierce* was revolutionary in so many ways, *Superconscious intuition* goes even further because of the intensive work that the Institute does to mature the understanding of intuition and its role in our consciousness awakening.

Part One presents the knowledge and insights I wish every person starting on their intuition development journey received. With a deeper understanding of the Universal Laws, the science that explains the functioning of intuition, and a grounding in the nature of Consciousness, we would avoid the traps and pitfalls of a superficial intuition.

Part Two offers the evolution of intuition development. But I want to be clear. This is not another intuition development guide, although the teachings provided here will wildly increase our intuition. It is a radical evolution in what we believe intuition to be, why we develop it and what it will truly bring to our lives if we dare to follow it all the way through.

Part Three challenges (even more) some of the most tightly held fixations we have about intuition that keep us playing in littleness instead of revolutionising our lives with the glory of our superconsciousness.

# What is superconscious intuition?

Superconscious intuition is the deepest phase of intuition. It is the phase in which we attune to the God Mind. It is the phase we access when we are in the state of being of Intuitive Intelligence.

In *Spiritually Fierce,* I introduced the concept of Intuitive Intelligence, which is the Institute's pioneering approach to developing intuition. The formula for Intuitive Intelligence is:

**Innate intuition + spiritual fierceness = Intuitive Intelligence**

Since that time, I have refined and expanded this definition. I now define Intuitive Intelligence as:

**An embodied state of being, which is nonlocal, acausal, active, participatory, deep, creative, and surrendered. All this combines to allow us to access superconsciousness.**

We unpack all of this throughout the book but put simply, Intuitive Intelligence is a *state of being* that allows us the clearest access to our highest form of intuition, superconscious intuition.

Superconscious intuition is a spiritually mature form of intuition that operates through nonlocality and acausality. In other words, it is a function of the quantum universe. It is active and participatory because it must be trained and cultivated. When we commit to developing our Intuitive Intelligence, we can access deep states of intuition that speak directly to our soul purpose. Intuitive Intelligence is the phase of intuition that creates reality rather than reacting to it. Yet, within this creative relationship, we understand ultimately that we surrender to God's will.

13

All intuition is the language of consciousness. Superconscious intuition is the consciousness of the God Mind. When we are in the state of Intuitive Intelligence, connected to our superconscious intuition, we are congruent with our highest truth and aligned with the immutable laws governing all consciousness's functioning.

## Local and nonlocal dimensions of consciousness

Embodying Intuitive Intelligence is breaking the habit of believing that we are human alone. We are, as a collective, addicted to this thought. We are addicted to limits we haven't even chosen to place on ourselves but have inherited. I call these borrowed limits. Subconsciously, we're addicted to thinking that we are finite and limited and that the problems we have in our lives we can only answer through the dominant local reality. But it's only dominant because we've most often placed our attention there.

Now we're choosing to place our attention somewhere very, very different. We're choosing to focus on the subtle reality that exists outside of, and paradoxically inside, local reality. We can call this nonlocal reality. What happens at nonlocal reality that makes superconsciousness so accessible?

At nonlocal reality, we are more energy than we are matter. Less solid, more wave-like motion. What that means is that we're more potential and less fact. What we are is not solid and fixed, and therefore we are much more easily changed. We can investigate our limits and surrender them in the same breath. We do not have to work through the dimensions of time and space to bring ourselves into the miracle. The miracle is always the same. It is overcoming the belief in separation to return to

14

the God Mind, to superconsciousness, to that place where all that ever was and ever will be exists.

## Local and nonlocal intuition

Just as there is not one dimension of consciousness, there is not ONE intuition. There are *intuitions*. We have two major forms of intuition – local and nonlocal. My work focuses on nonlocal intuition, so most of this book is dedicated to understanding that category of intuition. But it is worth understanding local intuition as we operate from both local and nonlocal intuitions at all times.

Our local intuition is biological and informed by our electrical-magnetic composition. We are electromagnetic beings that produce energetic fields. We are sensitive to one another's energy and the energy of everything around us. Energetic sensitivity refers to the 'ability of our body and nervous system to detect electromagnetic and other types of energetic signals in the environment'[2], according to the HeartMath Institute.

We are all empathic and highly sensitive, and when we understand our electromagnetic biology, it becomes clear why. We are constantly collecting energetic information from one another, most often without realising it. When we live the Intuitive Intelligence path, there are powerful ways that this energetic sensitivity can be part of our toolkit for living in extraordinary times. Rather than being something that makes us too sensitive to inhabit the world, we begin to understand the information provided to us through this kind of intuition and

---

2 HeartMath Institute, *Science of the Heart*, 2016. Acc: https://www.heartmath.org/research/science-of-the-heart/energetic-communication/

how to use it to our advantage. Local intuition is innate, primary and biological.

Nonlocal intuition is a type of intuition 'which refers to the knowledge or sense of something that cannot be explained by past or forgotten knowledge or by sensing environmental signals. It has been suggested that the capacity to receive and process information about nonlocal events appears to be a property of all physical and biological organisation, and this likely is because of an inherent interconnectedness of everything in the universe.[3]'

We explore the science and practice of nonlocal intuition throughout the book. Nonlocal intuition is the path of Intuitive Intelligence that leads us to superconsciousness.

## The dream of Earth School

The soul is singular in its purpose: to awaken to itself at deeper and deeper levels. We come into this consciousness experiment called life and land on Earth School to forget so we can remember. Every go-round that we have on Earth school, which is this local projection we're inhabiting, and part of the consciousness experiment in which we are all participating, is an opportunity to deepen into our truth that we are God. We do this repeatedly until we finally break free of the habit of believing that we are single, finite, fragile isolated humans with no capacity to change our lives. Until we meet ourselves as God, we will keep returning to the dream of Earth school.

The consciousness experiment of our lived experience is a dream.

---

3 Ibid, Acc: https://www.heartmath.org/research/science-of-the-heart/intuition-research/

When I speak of the dream, I'm talking about the beautiful, necessary illusion of local reality. I don't speak of it as an illusion to try to undermine it or to in any way reduce its importance for us. But instead, the dream of this life is a consciousness experiment. We can enter superconsciousness by productively engaging with the illusion of this blessed dream life.

This matters to this discussion of intuition because intuition is the language of consciousness. Much of the available intuition development teaches us how to engage with the dream. We are not intended to use intuition to 'move furniture in a burning building[4]', to quote Gary Renard referencing the teachings of *A Course in Miracles*. Instead, we must learn how to use our intuition to exit the burning building. We must activate our highest form of intuition to facilitate the awakening to the truth of what we are.

## What's God got to do with it?

Let us make a slight detour here if that word *God* causes any resistance or hesitation.

For here's the truth. Unless we are willing to accept that we are God, we will not inhabit our gloriousness. But it is impossible to accept ourselves as God if we have many competing, pre-existing ideas about what God is.

So what is God?

---

4 'Make no mistake: There's a difference in levels between this and other teachings. The rest of them are moving things around in a universe that isn't really there. That's like moving the furniture around in a burning house. Yes, it might look nice for a little while, but it's denying the real problem. A Course in Miracles, on the other hand, is the undoing of all of it, and the return to the only thing that is real.' *Your Immortal Reality*, Gary Renard

God is infinite, unlimited consciousness. God is everything. God is not human. Not male. Not religious or belonging to any religion. Not on a throne in the sky waiting to smite us down. Not keeping a scorecard. Not judging. Not condemning. Not separate from us. God is not what we believe. Most importantly, we do not have to earn our Godliness (or gloriousness), for it is what we are.

We are God.

In the following pages, I guide us through the changes in perception I have made and the practices I have used to give up my fear that I am not God and that I am not glorious, to move to a state of being that is willing to see the truth. Some days I get it; some days, I don't. A particular quality is required to break habits of lifetimes — conviction — which we will learn together now because the outcome is worth the effort.

## The Hermetic Laws

The Hermetic Laws continue to inform my understanding of the true functioning of intuition and are referenced consistently throughout this book. Let me provide a summary overview of the three immutable laws.

The theory and practices of Intuitive Intelligence assemble around the three immutable Hermetic laws — the law of mentalism, correspondence and vibration. The laws draw from *The Kybalion*: Hermetic Philosophy, originally published in 1908 under the pseudonym of the Three Initiates. This text contains the essence of the teachings of Hermes Trismegistus, also known as Thoth in Hellenistic Egypt. Thoth and Hermes were gods of writing and magic in their respective cultures. This information was handed down through secret orders over those thousands of years. Eventually, whether we believe by individuals or some higher power, it was agreed that this knowledge should be made public.

Around the 1930s, there was a significant appetite for an increased understanding of the occult laws and the things previously hidden from public view like Hermeticism and Rosicrucianism. There was a growing appetite for understanding how these laws were applied. A veil was lifted, and we could see much more clearly how the cosmos or the God Mind operated.

Today, we understand that it is not about just bringing the projection, the local reality or the illusion into a higher order. It's being able to see beyond it, to see the world within the world. This is really what the laws do. They lift our gaze from human sight up to that universal sight to think like the universe. The laws open us to the deeper spiritual meaning of our lives.

## What is a trinket and superstition of the new age?

One of the things that I've worked to change is the contemporary superficial spiritual training around intuition, which is so often about reliance on external tools and the externalisation of our power. We end up imagining that without special conditions — the crystal grid in our workroom, the energetic protection, the unique pendulum or even the idea of asking a question of our intuition — we cannot receive our intuition. This is intuition in its shadow form because it's undermining what intuition truly is.

It is not a matter of,

*I tune into my intuition to ask a question; I tune out of my intuition.*

We are our intuition, and our intuition is us. We live in flow with our superconscious intuition at all times, but mostly we are not aware of it. There's no coming in and going out again in a spiritually mature relationship with intuition. There are no cards to draw. There are no pendulums to swing. There is no one to ask. There's nothing except for,

*Am I congruent with the truth?*

And that truth is a flow state, and we will know it by how it feels to inhabit that state.

We're moving beyond,

*I'm going to tune in and ask God if I should marry that boy or if I should buy that house, or if I should invest in toilet paper stocks right now.*

We're not trying to organise the dream because when we connect to superconscious intuition, we move beyond the belief that local reality is the highest reality. Instead, we are learning our true nature. Sometimes, it works for half an hour at a time; sometimes for five minutes, sometimes we could do it for a whole day. We're learning to privilege our nonlocal non-dominant reality before the local because the local is secondary to the nonlocal. Consciousness precedes matter.

This book has been a long time coming — longer than I ever imagined. The world irrevocably changed in the wake of the COVID-19 Pandemic that began in 2020. At the time of writing, the pandemic still impacts all of our realities. I have found myself in a time of radical personal transformation, and for a while, the most profound service I could engage with was to hang myself on the hook of my being as I descended to the underworld/subconscious.

I am not alone in having been altered by the crisis/opportunity this seismic global change has wrought. It is the ground for our revolution, and the revolution we need more than any other is spiritual. When we are reconnected to our holiness, through reconnection to the language of our divinity — intuition — then all the other corrupt, outmoded and failing systems will be brought to their knees. This will happen because we as a collective have finally remembered who we are and will no longer accept the nightmare of separation consciousness. The contents of this book are the medicine I have returned to again and again to navigate these extraordinary times, and I am confident that this deepening, maturing relationship with our spiritual superpower will serve our awakening just as potently.

# PART ONE: FOUNDATIONS

*Dear God,*
*Encode me*
*Imprint me*
*Engineer me in your image*
*I am yours*
*And so it is.*
*And it is so.*

# Chapter 1

# The Laws of Superconsciousness

*"Truly I tell you, if anyone says to this mountain, 'Go, throw yourself into the sea,' and does not doubt in their heart but believes that what they say will happen, it will be done for them".*

—*Mark 11: 23 NIV*

I don't recall how I found the Hermetic Laws, but it was in the research phase of my first book, *Spiritually Fierce*. I sought a metatheory to better frame what I wanted to share about intuition. There are many spiritual laws bandied about, but the three immutable laws are the origin for most of them and captivated me from the first moment I found them. How had I not known about these laws? They explain everything. I suddenly had a framework not just for my investigation of intuition but for my spiritual life as a whole.

I felt an instant affinity and deep understanding of these laws. Everything I wanted to articulate about my spiritual path was evidenced in them. They cut through all the nonsense and noise of much contemporary spirituality. I sighed as I read, 'Once you understand, apply and align yourself with these

Universal Laws, you will experience transformation in every area of your life beyond what you have ever dared to imagine. The governing Laws seek neither to punish nor reward you. They are impersonal, operating automatically along unconscious lines without your conscious participation'[5].

The relief came that such a simple yet compelling understanding existed and that it was available for all seekers to access. Why do we make spirituality so superficial and unnecessarily complex, I wondered, when we have the truth laid out so plainly? In reading the *Kybalion* it solidified for me my efforts to strip my intuition training back to articulate only the truth contained in these laws. The discovery of these was like a firm handshake from God assuring me I was on the right path. Nothing about the development of our intuition had to be laden with the grandiosity of performative spirituality. I felt free, finally, to teach what was in my heart.

Intuitive Intelligence is ultimately opening to our God nature. We must know how the God Mind operates to activate our superconscious intuition. This is what the laws are. The laws give us the means to make sense of the apparent inconsistencies of our lives and view the events we experience with a universal perspective. This is a vital step in spiritual maturing and spiritual agency. Spiritual maturity is demonstrated in our ability not to take everything personally, and with this maturing comes the embodied state of Intuitive Intelligence. The three immutable laws explain the functioning of superconscious intuition. When we live in accord with these laws, we undoubtedly align with our highest form of intelligence in all moments of life. So let's explore them

---

5 Accessed at: https://www.mind-your-reality.com/seven_universal_laws.html. You can access the Kybalion for free here: https://www.google.com.au/books/edition/The_Kybalion/8sVEEAAAQBAJ?hl=en&gbpv=1&printsec=frontcover

# The Law of Mentalism

All is One. All is of the Mind.

The law of mentalism sounds like a very lofty law, but it is very straightforward. This principle embodies the understanding that everything in the Universe creates by thought. There is nothing in the Universe where this is not the case. The great law of spiritual psychology is that our thought or belief creates our reality. Everything that exists is energy: matter densified energy; energy is just refined matter. All is just energy.

The idea of the holograph is applicable here, which we will explore more of in Chapter Two. I'll keep it simple: all parts contain the whole in a holographic image. So it goes with the law of mentalism. When the law states that all is of the mind, we can conceive of this as both the one mind – or the mind of God – as well as our individual minds. Even now, we can glean a clue of how the spiritual paradox is at work here. We are one with the mind of God, and nothing exists that is not. We reside in the God Mind, and everything we live is a projection of that God-consciousness. Why the suffering, we may ask? If we reside in the mind of the benevolent Universe, then how could anything be less than love? Well, herein lies the paradox of spirituality. Within the Superconscious Mind, we have free will. Our choices and beliefs with which we seed our consciousness determine how our piece of reality appears. We can live inside the one mind of God and experience a living hell. Our power to create through our consciousness makes us what we are – divinity itself. Our humanness makes us forget that power or use it with such hit and miss results.

Everything that we are living in is a projection of our consciousness. It is what we are holding in our consciousness that is shaping reality. If we want to see a different reality and inhabit a different world, we need to change our minds about ourselves and the nature of the world in which we live. This takes great spiritual maturity not to take everything personally.

When we have these laws to lean into, we can start to move beyond the personal, beyond the immediate need for release or relief from our lives' conditions and see our soul's trajectory for what it is: vast, ancient, and magnificent. We are not asked to give up more than we will gain – ever. But in the moment, we may not be able to see beyond our suffering to what is on offer. We may not understand that we indeed created it, for this is what the laws teach us.

We also can choose not to become the full expression of the God Mind. Let's repeat that in another way. We do not lack anything. We are the same substance as God. We are the same substance as that which created everything. We possess that same capacity and power, but we have free will, our divine birthright, and whether we will fully express it.

There is an important caveat to this. The immutable cosmic truth is that, yes, we ARE all one. Yet, that is not the starting point. We must earn the right to claim that truth. We must look to our own subconscious biases, familial programming, cultural conditioning, and inherited fear programs.

In 2018, I discovered that I was a white supremacist. For an educated, well-travelled, spiritual and seemingly loving person, this was as shocking a discovery as it sounds. To keep it simple, my awakening began with Layla Saad, black feminist writer, racial justice advocate and spiritual thought-leader. Layla was educating white spiritual women to understand how our collective and individual behaviour was causing direct and real harm to black, brown, indigenous women of colour, through white supremacy, privilege, fragility, and exceptionalism. Layla offered a challenge on her Instagram that invited white women to address their inherent racism[6].

To start, please know I was deeply offended. I tried to count myself out of her accusations, and then I got angry. How dare she tell me that my spirituality was superficial, bypassing and violent? That wasn't me. She must be talking about other spiritual white women. I went through all the stages that I can see now were my ego attempts to maintain its power and privilege, and mostly its exclusion from the problem. Then at some point, as I kept meeting and unpacking this fear, I could feel my resistance melting.

Through investigating my subconscious programs, I could see that I was afraid of losing control. I was scared of looking foolish. How could I have been so blind? All my life, I have been on the path of spiritual seeking, to raise my consciousness — to be Oneness. Yet, this festering wound of separation was sitting right there in my subconscious, unnoticed. Unnoticed because the systems of power in the world privilege me as a white person, so I did not see what was in plain sight. It was a shocking and overdue awakening, and it altered me like few things before it had. Engaging with the politics of race initiated me into my sacred heart more readily than any spiritual program or text could have done. I did not anticipate that this would crack open my heart. But of course, it did.

The fear in the world is an illusion because local reality is an illusion. But it is a necessary illusion, for it is how we train our consciousness. That is the very purpose of incarnating on

---

6 This is now a best-selling book, and I encourage every white woman to buy it and to take the challenge https://www.meandwhitesupremacybook.com/ especially if the terms mentioned above are new to you. It is our responsibility to educate ourselves.

Earth School and the very function of fear. I don't say fear is an illusion so we can bypass other people's experiences, but instead, we will recognise that we have everything we need to meet it (we'll unpack this more in Chapter Four). The illusory nature of fear doesn't give us an opt-out in having to participate in the world's very real problems. What has created racism and all other social injustices is fear. And what will end the systemic injustices of the world is our willingness to go and meet that fear fearlessly, without thought for what we might lose, because we have already lost if we think we can attain enlightenment alone. We cannot. We are One Mind. And all must be returned to that state for anyone to return to that state.

We must take the time to understand what we are arrived of. Sit with God and let that energy move our souls so that we may meet the places we have been holding ourselves back from love because any block to love for another is us saying no to our superconsciousness. We must crave union with all life; let's turn our hearts back on. We must do the work to free consciousness collectively because we cannot be free in isolation.

## The Law of Correspondence

As above, so below; as within, so without.

The second law is the law of correspondence. The law of correspondence means that the thoughts and images we hold in our conscious and subconscious mind will manifest their exact likeness in our external reality. The outer world is a reflection of what is within us. Like all the cosmic laws, this law is impartial and works unceasingly for the good or the bad. The law of correspondence requires that we know we are in partnership with God. In other words, we are not doing it alone. This requires absolute trust. There are a few steps before we can honestly know if we live per the law. The first is that we trust. The second condition for the law of correspondence to come into the right action is that we possess self-esteem.

We need our spiritual self-esteem for the law of correspondence to work in our favour. Why does this law require us to trust God Consciousness? What does that have to do with self-esteem? Let's break it down: the law states that what we hold in our consciousness will manifest in the outer world. Remember that, as the law of mentalism tells us, consciousness is everything because all is of the mind. This makes sense when we apply it to the law of correspondence because it tells us that the inner and exterior are, in fact, one. The trust we need to feel in our God Consciousness is trust in ourselves because we are that – we are God. Trusting the God Mind is one condition of adhering to the law of correspondence.

Then there is the other condition, often more tricky, especially for spiritual seekers. Conceptually, we can say,

*I trust God.*

We are pretty prepared to believe that God has our back. We even potentially want to remember that we are God. Until we have met our fears of unworthiness, we cannot indeed partner with what we are, with our God nature. We are paying lip service to the idea and remain in fear in reality. As within, so without is another way of thinking about this law. We cannot say that we believe that God is all-powerful and deny that we are that power – breaking the law. The law of correspondence brings us to the inevitable truth that we are divine beings with finite human experience. We will suffer whilst we believe that we are a limited human consciousness because our true nature is trying to correspond or communicate *with itself* through this experience called life. Our mortal fear is thwarting those attempts. When we can forgo our limited belief, we begin to see our lives flourish because the truth of what we are can communicate clearly with itself on all planes, within and without, above and below.

We think we want to own our self-worth, but with that worthiness comes the responsibility for our superconscious power. More often than not, we run from our power. We think everyone else is responsible for the state of our lives, or is better than us, or didn't have the experiences we had and therefore can shine. The responsibility of being all-powerful means that we must ultimately surrender our human frailty. We have to trust that our lives have not gone astray, and, most importantly, we must stop blaming God for what has happened to us or what we see around us in the world. We must surrender our fear that we are not God. Or we must surrender our worry that we are God. The brilliant and sneaky ego has a million stories to keep us playing small. If we want to save the world, we must surrender our fear and meet ourselves as God Consciousness. As within, so without.

## The Law of Correspondence as a communication hotline

Intuitive intelligence is simply a symptom of a healed mind. The healing that occurs when we activate our Intuitive Intelligence corrects the false belief in separation and removes the blocks to our knowledge that we are in partnership with God Consciousness. God contains everything within it. It stands to reason that if we are connected and communicating with God-consciousness, which is all, then we have it all. Not only that, we have the means by which to draw it to us. An activated

Intuitive Intelligence is the most powerful manifestation tool we have. We draw towards us what corresponds to us. Another way to think about the law of correspondence is *communication*.

*What conversation am I having with myself and with God? Am I telling myself the world is a scary place full of dangerous people? Am I telling myself that I am worthless, nothing, weak and vulnerable?*

That communication is a direct command to the Superconscious Mind, and because we are Superconscious, the communication hotline is precise and robust. We are speaking (or thinking or feeling) our fears into reality. Communication is always happening, and as we understand from the levels of the mind, it is most often subconsciously calling the superconscious consciousness into action. The Superconscious Mind corresponds to communication because we are that powerful. How do we heal this faulty feedback loop? The power of knowing ourselves, particularly the contents of our subconscious mind, is the most crucial step to living by this law.

We need to wrap our heads around the idea of correspondence as communication. The Superconscious Mind doesn't simply correspond to our belief about it. It does it with direct intent. It does so we can overcome the faulty assumption of separation. Our true nature is Infinite and all-powerful, and anything in our lives that doesn't reflect that is an imbalance that will keep revisiting us until we correct it. It is a communication loop designed to bring us back into correspondence with our true nature. God isn't testing us – it is impartial. Everything in our lives, within and without, works to support our awakening so that when we have forgotten, the events we create from that forgetting will bring us home to ourselves.

*Can I believe that the Superconscious Mind is all-powerful and my partner and sit in feelings of low self-worth?*

No. We are breaking the law. The Universe will behave as per our belief. As within, so without. In this case, life will seem like a living hell, and God will appear to be punishing or testing us at every turn. As we know that this is not possible in truth, we have to look to ourselves. How can we heal the belief in separation, the dualism that makes us think that God's power is separate from us, and heaven is a place we can only access when we die? Living Intuitive Intelligence is the answer. And yes, it takes practice. Intuitive intelligence is remembering that we are a divine piece of a benevolent God.

## The Law of Vibration

The law of vibration is fascinating because, perhaps more than any others, the changes we see in our lives are radical and immediate when used consistently. We talk about changing our vibration a lot in spiritual circles. We're looking at the way that the big lofty, noble ideas of quantum physics can come into an applied or practical application in our own lives.

The principle of this law explains the difference between the manifestations of matter and energy and how there is no actual difference. Every atom and molecule is vibrating in a particular motion. The motion is the shape of the Torus. Science has been telling us for more than 100 years now that everything is energy and that we are part of a unified consciousness or quantum field.

Globally, we have not taken on this knowledge because it terrifies us.

*What if I AM one with all that there is? What if my vibration IS informing superconsciousness and telling it how to behave? Am I manufacturing my existence through my consciousness? Primarily through my unmet or unknown subconscious mind?*

This law is premised on energy first, physical second. It's this connection that makes deep states of intuition between people and patterns between significant life events possible. This is what I postulate when we talk about the law of mentalism. When we get to the law of vibration, it becomes very applied.

No matter how it appears through the dominant senses, quantum physics confirms that we are not solid matter at all. The reason that we believe in our solid matter above our energy state is that we're lazy. It's straightforward to see local reality through our dominant senses. It's much harder to perceive ourselves as our quantum or energetic nature.

We default to the physical reality, the local reality, because we can see it right in front of us. It takes training to understand that our true nature is energetic and that our energy body is far vaster than our physical body. Our physical body is, in fact, just part of our energy field. Our physical bodies are atoms vibrating at a slower frequency and are therefore much denser and more able to be perceived through the dominant five senses. This is not the full expression of what we are. What we've seen in the mirror has very little to do with what we are and from where we're creating. In particular, we expand our field when we do our devotional practices. We take ourselves into a higher vibrational state. There's no limit to what we can do when releasing our fear with our God-consciousness.

What expands our energy body? What raises our vibration? What slows it down? The feeling state that we hold determines the frequency at which our particles are moving.

Feeling as frequency moves through the physical body but generates at the energetic level. The prayer sits in the heart, which is the centre that connects us to the Superconscious Mind. The law of correspondence could also be called the law of communication. We communicate with that Superconscious field, but we also receive from the Superconscious field. What determines that exchange is the frequency that we're holding.

Let's break it down a little bit. When we look at quantum physics, we know that we are energy first and physical second. The physical appears per the energetic vibration. We talked a little bit before about the idea that everything is in its pure energetic state until we place our gaze or attention upon it. This was proven in the double-slit experiment, which was first done in the 19th century. This experiment has been repeated with the same outcome many times since then.

What happens in an untrained consciousness is that we think that the events of local reality determine our vibration. If I have a good day and my children behave well, get a pay rise, and my boss is pleasant, I'll feel good about myself and hold a higher vibration. Conversely, if I'm having a rubbish day and get a parking ticket and don't get what I want in work or my relationship, I am entitled to sit in my lower vibrations, my low feeling states. Then I perceive my life as a reaction to external circumstances.

The law of vibration shows us that our external circumstances exist only to reflect the frequency that we're holding. It is always up to us to determine the choice and the vibration we hold via our feeling state. If I choose to experience a high vibrational feeling state, even if local reality is not behaving itself, I am starting to craft the world I want to live in.

The next step along the path of creating from feeling means we go from passively waiting for God to give us what we need to generate what we need for ourselves (through the recognition that we are God!). That's a genuinely magnificent state of being. It requires a commitment to practice holding the highest vibrational feeling states, even when the local reality isn't behaving itself.

We're trying to effectively unite the physical level of our vibrating particles with our energy level, with our Superconscious Mind. We're trying to imbue the superconscious into the energy body so that the physical body can show up in a much higher vibration. At the physical level, we need to regulate the nervous system. The nervous system is the repository holding the history of our experiences. Until we regulate the nervous system, or in other words neutralise the emotional charge of our memories, we're not going to be able to hold this higher vibrational state. We can't just change our conscious reasoning mind, hoping to change our nervous system or anything else. We need to go to the subconscious program.

The nervous system controls the limbic brain or the subconscious level of mind. It is holding a different feeling that will alter our consciousness. Remember, our physical body is only a reflection or an aspect of our energy body. Our energy body is in communion with our soul body. The less fear we hold in our energy body, the more we hear our intuition. We're beginning to see how this happens, how both the energy and physical bodies need to come into congruence to open to our superconscious intuition. The result of that, of course, is that we live in heaven on earth. We do not live in a state of despair; we do not live in a nightmare any longer.

We must practice holding a greater state of being than our external circumstances. It doesn't matter how magnificent our life is or how rubbish it is; we can go further into that experience of heaven on earth by cultivating the practice of holding a higher vibration or a higher state of being than our external circumstances warrant. The holding of that new vibration shifts us out of survival mode and into an expanded state. That expansion is happening at the level of energy. We are growing our size. We're moving from this tightly wound, tightly held fear-based organism into an expanded state where we move out and fill up space. We can easily decode the information of the Superconscious Mind far more readily in our expanded form.

This is an exciting understanding because it puts the power so squarely in our hands. We always have a choice about how we feel. The more frequently we choose to hold a higher vibration, the more powerfully we can change our external reality. We understand then. It's the law that when we feel it, we will receive it. We can make change not by holding on to current fears but by holding a vibration that is disproportionate or greater than our current reality. In doing so, we bring a new reality. We bring the miracle into our lives.

I want to share a story from my own life with you, illustrating these three laws in action. The months before my marriage ended, I felt deeply unsatisfied with the relationship, but I didn't yet feel confident of the next best step. I set myself the task of *encoding consciousness*. I didn't know how things should be, but I knew how they should feel. So here's what I did.

I recognised that I wanted only the highest outcome for my husband and myself. Whenever I strayed into judgement or blame towards him, I corrected myself to the truth that he is me. All is one.

What I saw in him was also in me. I avoided blame and shame in this way. I could only be seeing any perceived shortcomings in him because, in some way, they existed in me and because they were the perfect elements to support my awakening. Whatever I was offering him in terms of the quality of my communication and my emotional and energetic attitude towards him, I could expect to receive back in return. So I never closed my heart to him, even though we were both scared and confused —as within so without.

I took responsibility for the future created for us both at the level of pure consciousness by spending time in my devotion each day, feeling the highest outcome fulfilled, and for all impediments and problems to be melted away. The way I did this was to focus on a symbol that represents freedom, joy, expansion, gratitude and ease. This symbol was the letter 'p', which means *problemlessness*. I felt so profoundly in each meditation that whatever came next for us and our relationship would be no problem. I felt it totally and completely with daily consistency for months. I didn't try to figure out what that would look like. I just held the truth that everything is a vibration, and I accepted only this vibrational frequency of *problemlessness*. As you recall from the preface, that's precisely the outcome we both received.

# Chapter 2

# The Science of Superconsciousness

*"God is the ceaseless longing to become all that you can be".*

—Pam Grout

Is there a way to have a conversation about intuition that goes beyond spiritual trinkets and superstitions? When we look to science, there is. Our innate ability to understand and connect with one another beyond the dominant five senses – in other words, to activate our Intuitive Intelligence — is explained by science in many ways, but I want to share two key areas that demonstrate how our biology is the technology of our intuition.

One. Intuitive Intelligence is an intelligence based on; the inherent interconnectedness of all consciousness and; our capacity to attune to nonlocal and acausal consciousness with focussed intention and attention. We produce electro-magnetic fields made up of vibrating particles that communicate with everything around us beyond our physical limits because of this fact.

Two. We have a little brain in our heart, which sends more information to the brain than the other way around. Intuitive intelligence is a function of the heart-brain, a cluster of 40,000 neural cells in the anatomical heart that is precognisant and with an electromagnetic field 500 times greater than the cranial brain.

As a result of these two biological premises, we have access to Intuitive Intelligence, which simultaneously contributes to self-reliance and a deep sense of connection to others. How is that so? Let's look at the science.

At the quantum level, subatomic particles are ripples in an electromagnetic field. The ripples create those fields. Subatomic particles, which are not particles but waves of motion, move in a field. Everything generates a field from the subatomic particle to the entire universe. We are fields, within fields, within fields. These fields of motion influence everything around us. Our field is influencing the field of the Universe and the field of the person next to us. We know that there is a unified field connecting everything. We can learn to actively connect with this nonlocal field to guide our lives and have access to the information we need at any moment.

We do this by learning to privilege our heart brain. Our heart is the communication portal to the quantum field because it generates the largest electromagnetic field of any part of the human body. The heart is so much more than a muscle that pumps blood.

When a new life is conceived in utero, something remarkable happens around day 17 of gestation. A cluster of cells appears from somewhere in the womb that moves into the primitive kidney bean shape of the new life forming, down the primitive space that will become the throat. This small cluster of cells moves into the primitive branches of what will become the lungs, and the heartbeat begins. There has been a lot of research about what signals the body to start producing a heart. It has been discovered that the heart is not normal cells, but something called ID proteins, and ID proteins are not DNA. They do not come from mum. They do not come from dad.

They are protein cells that have no genetic makeup. There's nothing in them that says, 'Become a heart,' like all the other cells that express, 'Become a finger, become a kidney, become a toe.' They're random proteins, and their job is to be the glue. They take other cells in the body and glue them together to create the heart. Scientists have no idea from where the ID protein originates. It's not in eggs. It's not in sperm. All that is known is that they come from the environment in which the embryo is growing. ID proteins come from the womb. They come from the uterine space and only when an embryo needs a heart. We cannot go into the uterus and harvest ID proteins when a woman is not pregnant. They are only generated by the womb when an embryo requires a heart[7].

Our heart is our connection with our nonlocal intuition. Our heart is not an anatomical pump that pumps blood around our body because blood has its own propulsion mechanism. The heart simply does not have enough size to move all the blood around required for a human to function. Our heart, we know, is our connection to the God Mind. It's where we go to tap into all of this. And its origins are truly mystical.

The heart is the bridge between the local and nonlocal fields. It possesses a profound and undervalued form of intelligence. The electrical signal produced by the heart is a hundred times stronger than any other part of our body because of all the electrical conductivity that happens in the heart. The

---

7 This information was shared with me by midwife and yoni massage practitioner trainer, Amy Towle, of Temple of She.

heart's magnetic field is 100 times bigger than the field produced by the brain. We're seeing that our inbuilt biology is primed at the centre to attune us to the one mind more effectively than any other part of our physical anatomy. The heart-brain is the best point of connectivity to that one mind, to that field that contains all information.

In a study by HeartMath's psycho-physiologist Rollin McCraty in 2004, it was found that a participant's heart rate significantly slowed before a future emotional picture was shown to the participant; that while both the heart and brain receive and respond to intuitive information, the heart appears to receive that information first. The HeartMath Institute study suggests that the heart is the main conduit that connects us to the quantum field and that it is the heart that then relays intuitive information to the brain, HearthMath Institute tells us.

HeartMath researcher Raymond Bradley designed experiments to understand the success of repeat entrepreneurs. The study discovered that the entrepreneur's passionately focused attention directed to an object of interest (e.g., a future business opportunity) attuned the bio-emotional energy generated by the body's psychophysiological systems to a domain of quantum-holographical information, which contains implicit, energetically-encoded information.[8]

In layman's terms, this means that when we focus our feeling state, we tune into a domain beyond the world of the senses, described here as 'quantum-holographic information', that contains information that is energetically encoded.

---

8 Raymond Bradley et al. (2015) Nonlocal Intuition in Entrepreneurs and Non-entrepreneurs: An Experimental Comparison Using Electrophysiological Measures. Access here: noosphere.princeton.edu/papers/pdf/bradley.intuition.2007.pdf

I recall a night several years ago when my son, now 15 years old, was terribly out of sorts. He was oppositional and angry and rejected all forms of attention and love. Eventually, as he crawled into bed, he said to me,

*I'm sad because something is wrong with Ebony.*

Ebony, his little sister, who lived across town with their dad and Finn's step-mother, had just been admitted to hospital with a severe infection of the salivary glands that caused her face and neck to swell and triggered a great deal of pain. Back at our house, we weren't yet privy to that information. But my son knew something was up. I sent his dad a message to console him and didn't think about it again.

The following day we found out that my son was, of course, right to be concerned. Ebony fully recovered, but this direct experience of my son's intuition left me deeply contemplative about the inherent interconnectedness of all consciousness. My son's love for his sister (passionately-focused attention) gave him access to knowledge about his sister nonlocally (quantum-holographical information) that had not yet been shared with us locally. The holographic nature of consciousness explains how my son could know what his sister was experiencing.

## The Holograph

'Man appears as a being whose primary level of existence is at non-space, non-time levels of the Universe, and who has placed himself in a space-time vehicle of consciousness for the purpose of growing in awareness of the True Self and generating coherence in the True Self. Our perception mechanisms at the space-time vehicle level lock us into a narrowly restricted view of reality and the Self. Disharmony created by the ego at the deeper level of self, materialises as error or disease in the space-time vehicle as an indicator that error has been created at a primary level …It teaches us that the space-time vehicle is not Life but only a simulator of Life whose only role is as a teaching tool. With our thoughts and attitudes, we continuously reprogram the simulator from the Mind level of the multidimensional universe and continuously generate our individual and collective futures by such behaviour."[9] —Dr William Tiller

The torus is the shape of the movement of the particle's motion. When we talk about vibrating particles, the shape of the torus is the shape it creates. Our subatomic particle produces that torus shape, the cell in our bodies produces that torus shape, our entire physical body produces that torus shape, and so does the whole universe. Everything has that same energetic signature. We are all creating the same shaped field. We understand that

---

9 Richard Gerber, *Vibrational Medicine*, 1988, p161-162

the vibration of the particle occurs because, at the subatomic level, there isn't a particle. That wave produces a field, and the field is the torus shape.

That field is holographic. The part contains the whole. To connect to the Superconscious mind is to say *we* are the Superconscious mind because *the part contains the whole*. The more expanded we are, the more relaxed and open, the more soft and receptive we are, the more we receive from that one mind, from that field. The more afraid and future-focused in a negative way and attached to the past, the more contracted we are. It becomes challenging for that infinite One mind to commune with us. We might desperately want our intuition to guide us because we're feeling so scared, but we've created a state of being that's at odds with our true nature, with the nature of the cosmos, which is open and expansive. We must learn how to control our state to create a coherent state between the heart and the cranial brains. Suppose we're in an incoherent or incongruent state. In that case, it is tough for us to be in that natural, expansive state of being that allows us to receive our Intuitive Intelligence from within.

The Einsteinian paradigm observes that humans are networks of complex energy fields that interface with physical/cellular systems. Einstein proved that energy and matter are dual expressions of the same universal substance. That universal substance is primal energy or vibration of which we are all composed. We direct this primal energy through consciousness. Richard Gerber, the author of the seminal text, *Vibrational Medicine*, states that 'consciousness itself is a kind of energy that is integrally related to the cellular expression of the physical body'[10].

---

10 In Richard, Gerber, *Vibrational Medicine*, 1988. p44

Joe Dispenza talks about this in terms of light and information or energy and consciousness. 'Everything in our known Universe is made up of or emits either light and information or energy and consciousness – which are other ways of describing electromagnetic energy…there's a sea of infinite, invisible frequencies that are carrying encoded information…All frequency carries information[11]'.This explains why we can access information nonlocally and outside of time and space. The holograph explains this even more so. From understanding the science of the holographic image, we know that every piece contains the whole. 'That is, one could take a hologram of an apple, cut the film into fifty pieces, and each piece, when viewed through laser light, would reveal its miniature apple[12]. Gerber relates the holographic principle to the hermetic law of as above, so below – the law of correspondence.

In *Vibrational Medicine,* it is also demonstrated that when the image of a tiny seedling is taken using electrography, the surrounding electrical field of the seedling is the shape of the adult plant. When a leaf is photographed with the top of the leaf intentionally removed, the full image of the leaf appears in the electrophotographic image. When a circular hole is cut into a leaf and then photographed, the image reveals a tiny intact leaf with a similar hole.

What is essential for us is that our biology is optimised at the level of the energy field to become the fullest expression of what it is. And no matter what occurs at the physical level, at the energy level, all that we are remains whole. What would it take for the energy field to return the physical to its full health

---

11 Joe Dispenza, *Becoming Supernatural*, 2017, p85

12 Richard, Gerber, *Vibrational Medicine*, 1988, p48

and expression? We are optimised to become the full expression of our superconscious nature. A correction in our perception is what makes this change possible.

Richard Gerber states it like this,

'Every piece of the universe contains information concerning the makeup of the entire cosmos. Unlike a static hologram, the cosmic hologram is a dynamically moving system that changes from microsecond to microsecond. Because what happens in just a small fragment of the holographic energy interference pattern affects the entire structure simultaneously, there is a tremendous interconnectivity relationship between all parts of the holographic universe. If one were to view God as "all there is", then, through the holographic interconnectivity of space, God could simultaneously be in contact with all creations'[13].

How we tap into the information, the superconsciousness enfolded into the structure of space, is to become congruent, and raise our vibration to a state in which our internal receiver is most finely tuned. We do that by understanding what level of consciousness we are paying attention to.

---

13 Richard Gerber, *Vibrational Medicine*, 1988, p61

# Chapter 3

# The Layers of Consciousness

*"The brain commands the behaviour of our physical body, but the mind commands the behaviour of our energy body, which is our relationship to thought and perception. The brain is the physical instrument through which thought is transferred into action, but perception – and all that is associated with perception, such as becoming conscious – is a characteristic of the mind. In becoming conscious, one is able to detach from subjective perceptions and see the truth or symbolic meaning in a situation. Detachment does not mean ceasing to care. It means stilling one's fear-driven voices".*

*Caroline Myss*

We use the term consciousness to describe the collection of beliefs we have, individually and collectively. Most of these beliefs are unconscious, inherited, tribal, and familial. The process of spiritual awakening is raising consciousness. We become aware of the contents of our subconscious as we awaken, and we raise our belief out of the darkness and into the light, so we may investigate its contents and release what we don't need. Sometimes it is becoming aware of the inherited program of racism, and sometimes the fear of abandonment. Other times it's deprogramming from a particular religion or reclaiming the word God from unhelpful dogma. Quite literally, we raise our beliefs from the subconscious to conscious, to eventually return to the understanding that we are part of one consciousness (the intentional descent to the underworld). That one consciousness is God.

As we raise our consciousness, we start to make choices,

*Do I want that in there?*

*Do I want to believe that old familiar bond, that old belief system that has been handed down from generation to generation?*

*Do I want to think about what my dominant cultural program tries to convince me of?*

*Do I want to be indoctrinated with ideas and knowledge that I didn't choose for myself?*

We investigate these beliefs as we raise our consciousness from the subconscious basement. We make better choices. We evolve our consciousness. But that isn't the end of the journey. We are raising our consciousness to, ultimately, return to the God Mind. We are raising our consciousness to the level of superconsciousness.

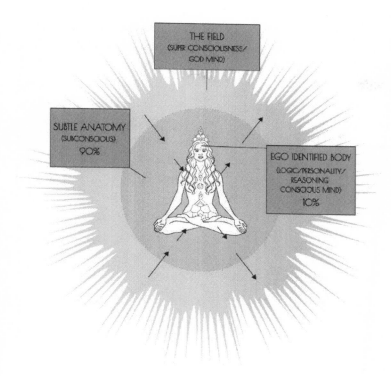

To explain the functioning of Intuitive Intelligence, we focus on a simple understanding of consciousness. For our purposes, we need to consider three aspects of consciousness — the Conscious Reasoning Mind, the subconscious mind, and the Superconscious Mind.

The **Reasoning Conscious Mind** is the 10% of the brain (at most) that expresses our personality into the world. Our conscious mind is what most people associate with who they are because most people live there day-to-day. It's by no means where all the action takes place.

Our conscious mind is like the captain of a ship standing on the bridge giving out orders. In reality, it's the crew in the engine room below deck (the subconscious) that carry out the orders. The captain may be in charge of the ship and give the orders, but the crew operates the ship.

We can think of the Reasoning Conscious Mind as the egoic mind. From a spiritual perspective, ego means considering oneself distinct from others and God due to identification with the physical body and impressions in various centres of the subtle body. In short, ego leads our life because our existence is limited to our five senses.

As the one and same superconsciousness exist within all, there is unity in all creation from a spiritual perspective. However, depending on the level of our ego, we identify with the Superconscious Mind to varying degrees. If our ego is high and concretised in our personality, we identify less with our superconsciousness.

The **subconscious** is the storehouse of all belief. The process of spiritual awakening is becoming conscious of the thoughts, fears, ideas, programs, traumas and identities harboured in our subconscious. We live from here 90% of the time.

I correlate the subconscious mind with the subtle anatomy. The subtle anatomy is the filter between the Superconscious Mind and the physical body. It is the filter through which we receive superconsciousness. The subtle anatomy/ subconscious is the interface between local and nonlocal (the thoughts, feelings and emotions that create the vibration we reside within). Anything blocking the filter of our subconscious/subtle anatomy will disrupt the proper flow of life force.

The **Superconscious Mind** is the God Mind, the unified field containing all time and space. All is one in the mind of God. It is unlimited, infinite consciousness.

Our ultimate aim is to have no impediment in the subtle anatomy between the Superconscious Mind and us, for this is our natural and most intuitive state of being. We would like to imagine that the Reasoning Mind, which we identify with our personality, our likes, and the things by which we define ourselves (I like jazz, I'm not too fond of sushi, etc.), is in charge. But it's not as simple as that. According to psychologist and author Venice Bloodworth, the relationship between the conscious and subconscious mind is like this:

'Every thought that enters the conscious mind is subjected to our reasoning power. If we accept an idea or thought as true, it is then carried forward to the subconscious mind to act on'[14].

Remember, the subconscious is beneath the deck yet is the most significant part of our consciousness. We are largely unaware of what is stored there. Bloodworth suggests that the subconscious is 'the marvellous phase of your mind that brings things into existence by the sheer power of thought'[15]. The subconscious mind is highly programmable, and because we have mostly not been aware that we are one with the Mind of God, we have believed our fear stories and the fear stories of the world around us. We have focused our attention on those things without any filter. The ship's captain, in other words, has looked this way and that, absorbed by the events of life and has passed very mixed instructions to the subconscious below deck.

---

14 Venice Bloodworth, Key to Yourself, 1952
15 ibid.

Combined with how our brain has evolved primed to identify danger in our environment, the result is that the bulk of our consciousness attunes to the negative, fear-based dominant consciousness of the collective reality we witness. We have forgotten that we are co-creating with the Superconscious Mind. Our access to the Superconscious Mind gets blocked because our subconscious is full of stuff we didn't even know we focused on. The result of this for our lives is chaos. Most of us live with a general sense of managed chaos, waiting for the next event or emotional storm to derail us. If the Mind is uninvestigated, if we have not taken the time to explore the contents below deck, then we cannot know the difference between our fear and intuition.

I have a dear and deeply spiritual friend. She offers wonderful, soulful advice whenever I seek it. But she seems woefully unaware of her patterns and the chaos she manufactures as a result. From what she has shared with me from her early life experience, it is clear that she has trauma stored in her subconscious, especially regarding negative self-worth programs. I have watched her as every time she reaches success in her service, and she unconsciously sabotages it. This has happened in many different ways.

Once, it was in reaction to perceived criticism from one of her clients. Within 24 hours of feeling the sting of this client's assessment of her, she had taken all her spiritual books and instruments and thrown them in the bin. Another time, as her business was taking off, she decided she had to move house and away from her growing client base. Yet another way this manifests is in the treatment of her own body, including overeating and indulging in the wrong foods, which has led to her being overweight and suffering from Type II Diabetes.

She is very insightful regarding limiting behaviours in myself and others, but she cannot observe them in herself, so she has not taken the time to correct the programs in her subconscious. Part of this is willful ignorance (we talk later about the dangers of denial), and part of it is that it is much easier to see subconscious behaviours in others than in ourselves. The antidote to this is to assume that everything I see in another is a reflection of what is within me. This is the law; all is one, after all. As we understand, everything is continually working to serve our awakening, so if I am witnessing something in another person, it is wise for me to ask,

*How is this playing out in my subconscious programs?*

## Subconscious Mind / Subtle Body Connection

"Everything is first worked out in the unseen before it is visible in the seen; in the ideal before it shows forth in the real; in the spiritual before it manifests in the material. Your subconscious mind is bringing you the matured fruits of your mental action."
—Dr Venice Bloodworth

The Subtle Anatomy (subconscious mind) is the filter between the nonlocal God Mind (superconsciousness) and the local mind (Reasoning Conscious Mind). The health of the subtle anatomy determines the health of the relationship of both the nonlocal and the local levels of consciousness. We can also look at this as; the health of the subconscious determines the health of the relationship with both superconsciousness and the Reasoning Conscious Mind. These are the three immutable laws at work.

The law of Mentalism states All is One, and we can evidence this here because, in truth, there is no separation between these three layers of Mind. When we are in optimal functioning, the veils are very thin between the local and the nonlocal. Ultimately, there is no separation. The thinner the veils between the layers, the more we receive our intuition.

We also witness the law of Correspondence in action, as within so without. As above, so below. We are in a constant communication loop from inner to outer and outer to inner. The more harmonious all the layers of Mind are with one another, the more our intuition flows into us. We are also aware that we are not acting in isolation. Within my subconscious is what I am contributing to the Superconscious Mind. To give is to receive, and we receive in accordance with the quality of what we are offering.

Fear contracts the subtle anatomy makes it denser, the veils thicker, and the frequency slower and lower. This is the law of Vibration in action. The frequency of the Superconscious Mind is high and light. Superconsciousness can most easily be accessed when we have the same frequency or vibration. The more I clear my subconscious (subtle anatomy), the easier it is for me to hold my vibration at the level of the Superconscious Mind. I am then more easily imprinted with the vibration of the Superconscious Mind, and my intuition flows into me.

Recently I had a big decision to make about where I was living. There were several options available to me, and whilst I knew something had to change about my situation, I couldn't get clear on whether or not I should move or change the way I was using the house. It felt like a difficult choice because it impacted my kids and their schooling. I usually make these decisions easily as I am in the flow state with my intuition. Change doesn't intimidate me at all. It is something I thrive on. Yet even that quality about me was making this decision harder.

Was I seeking change for change's sake because I was restless? I ended up seeking a bunch of different opinions. This is a definite red flag that indicates I am not in the state of being of my Intuitive Intelligence. I sought advice from wise counsel, but I still couldn't get clear even after that. I didn't take the time to regulate myself and slow my life down. This was undoubtedly the medicine I needed, but I was so caught up in my head that I couldn't see the wood for the trees.

A few days later, I decided and started the ball rolling to move house. Still, I felt restless. I thought not taking action was causing my agitation, but nothing changed. I was short-tempered and confused. I kept ploughing on, oblivious to the fact that I had contracted my subtle body through unmet fear. I was sitting in my own blindspot. The next night I had a series of vivid dreams. I woke up with absolute clarity. I am no dream expert, but I also know that only we can interpret our dreams' meaning. It was so clear that my Intuitive Intelligence had utilised my dream state to bypass my ego and get me the intel I needed. I didn't need to move. It wasn't the right time. Another, simpler solution was available. I stopped the ball rolling on moving, and certainty prevailed within me as soon as I did. The situation wasn't immediately resolved, but I was no longer in doubt, and I could see how I had hijacked myself with a dominant subconscious fear of lack. I took to work meeting that fear in my subtle body and making the inspired choices in my local reality with no more worry in my being.

# Chapter 4

# The Function of Fear

*"I am convinced that the deepest desire within each of us is to be liberated from the controlling influences of our own psychic madness or patterns of fear. All other things—the disdain of ordinary life, the need to control others rather than be controlled, the craving for material goods as a means of security and protection against the winds of chaos—are external props that serve as substitutes for the real battle, which is the one waged within the individual soul."*
—*Caroline Myss*

Intentionally meeting and releasing subconscious fear is how we prime the subtle body to become the clearest interface between the Superconscious Mind and us. Until we meet our subconscious fear directly, it will rule us. Yet, subconscious fear is only a problem if we do not engage with it. Intentional fear release is the only way to attain the embodied state of Intuitive Intelligence. This is because fear disrupts our natural state of grace by causing 'knots' in the subtle anatomy. These knots inhibit the free flow of life force. However, fear shows us where these blocks or knots exist, so fear is a friendly ally when we know how to work with it intentionally and productively.

The good news is we are primed to release fear. We simply have not known how to work with it. To increase our Intuitive Intelligence, we must make a bold choice to descend into the subconscious of our being. This is how we return to our holiness by being willing to be stripped of our illusory identity — the fear identified personality. Meeting our fear intentionally and consciously is an active choice to surrender illusion. We become nothing to become everything. We cannot ascend to the fullness of what we are — superconsciousness — if we have not met ALL of what we are, including our shadow.

I worked with a student who had decided to return to corporate work after not making a successful career in her spiritual business. At the time of our session, she was in a state of freeze, meaning that she wasn't looking for paid corporate work and wasn't trying to grow her spiritual client base. We talked through all the aspects of her situation for a few minutes, and we identified that saboteur archetype at work in her consciousness, manifesting as the procrastinator. She avoided showing up to her life to avoid the feeling of shame and disappointment about her business. The only antidote was to go and meet this energy and commune with it. I proposed that we move into an altered state of consciousness and access her subconscious to connect with the procrastinator archetype. My student is trained in this work and highly skilled at it, so it took very little time for her to access the moment in this lifetime when the archetypal energy took hold. She was around the age of 10 when she felt like a cloak of invisibility wrapped around her. It was associated with her stepping into womanhood. That time in her life triggered a feeling of being controlled and losing her freedom. She went into hiding in many ways energetically.

When we worked together to meet and release the subconscious program, and then we laid out some practical steps for her to take in local reality to anchor into the energetic changes we had made. These included stepping back into her spiritual business to give herself a chance to do so with the cloak of invisibility removed. We didn't need to know the highest outcome for her in local reality. It may be to attract more clients, or it might be better for her to find a fantastic corporate job. The only measure of success here is that my student is carrying less fear within her subtle body. This is the freedom she is seeking, and whatever she does with her time now will feel like freedom because of that.

We are made holy by becoming aware that light and dark, heaven and hell, above and below, are One. We must be willing to sit with the discomfort of meeting the fullness of our being — shadow and light — and to be stripped bare of the egoic adornments we have tried to use to protect ourselves.

There is a caveat to this. Intentional fear release is only truly possible in a regulated system. The regulation required is of the nervous system. In the second half of this book, we will explore nervous system regulation as we understand our biology is the technology of our Intuitive Intelligence. Nervous system regulation is not a one time deal. We move in and out of regulation every day. In Chapter Eight, we dive deep into this and explore creating the optimal conditions for receiving our Intuitive Intelligence.

In this chapter, we extend on the conversation that began in *Spiritually Fierce*, information about the capacity of subconscious fear to be both the impediment and access point to the state of being called Intuitive Intelligence.

We can look to the Hindu God, Ganesha, as a powerful symbol of how fear is both the problem and the solution in increasing our Intuitive Intelligence. We pray to Ganesha as the remover of obstacles. However, few realise that in another form, that of Vigneshwara, the elephant-headed God is also the one who places obstacles in the way! In another powerful parallel with our work, Ganesha's holy vehicle, which transports him through the celestial realms, is a mouse. What we know to be true about elephants is that they are terrified of mice! The only way for Ganesha to move is to ride his fear. And so it goes with us. Meeting our fear is the only way to evolve!

## The Anatomy of fear

There are two kinds of fear for our exploration; physiological fear and psychological fear. Physiological fear is our body's unconscious response to being in a situation against our survival. Our body kicks in with a fight, flight, freeze or fawn response. This is a function of the autonomic nervous system, and its design is to protect us from danger.

It alerts us when we are in danger and in a regulated system, provides the chemical instructions to survive that situation; a shot of adrenaline and cortisol, for example, when we are in the way of an oncoming vehicle, which gives us the energy to get out of the way very quickly. Breathing and heart rate increases, peripheral blood vessels — such as in the skin — constrict, central blood vessels around vital organs dilate to flood them with oxygen and nutrients, and our muscles are pumped with blood, ready to react. A fear response like this is justifiable when we are in danger. But this kind of fear response can also be inappropriate, such as when triggered when we are quietly reading a book or on our daily commute. Fear's essential role in our survival as a species means our system is often too easily aroused to fear. The amygdala is in the brain, which forms part of the limbic system, and is the brain's alarm system.

In many of us, the amygdala is triggered by *non-survival* matters. In other words, we go into a flight or fight response in mundane or even safe situations because that early warning system is over-reactive. This can happen when we live a life against our Intuitive Intelligence. We create a dysregulated system when we ignore our intuition for long enough and make choices against what we truly know is suitable for us. When we ignore our deeper needs long enough — such as not leaving the job we hate, not putting in good boundaries with a narcissistic parent, or dating emotionally unavailable people — our psychological fear tricks us into thinking it is a physiological response. The alarm in our brain goes off all the time, and we live in survival mode even when we are not in danger. Eventually, we don't know the difference, and we certainly don't know how to shut the brain alarm off.

We can then develop an addiction to the fear state, and it is, without question, the biggest impediment to clear access to our intuition, our actual state of wholeness and holiness. The body has become addicted to living in that heightened state. The body produces more and more cortisol and adrenaline for no apparent external reason. So the mind goes looking for a problem and inevitably will find something upon which to fixate. All of this moves us further and further away from the embodied state of Intuitive Intelligence.

Here's how we can begin to unpack that. The subconscious is a pure creative force. The subconscious mind is not primed for fear. It's just that we've programmed it with fear, and we've done it so consistently that the program runs below the level of the Reasoning Conscious Mind the majority of the time. Remember, the crew below deck, the subconscious, always accepts the Captain's orders. As the Captain, we have input faulty data by living lives against our divine nature. We have focussed on information that does not serve us. We have 'entertained' ourselves with fear. We have believed other people's negative opinions of us. We are obsessed with the negatives in our life.

We end up in a self-fulfilling loop with our fear. Paradoxically, we then attempt to flee from the discomfort of that fear-dominant life. We try to distract ourselves from the very thing we have indulged. This is when we are ripe for addiction — shopping, working, eating, drinking, television, social media, gossiping, emotional chaos — anything that offers temporary relief from the chaos below decks. We get further and further away from ourselves. We no longer know what we need. We certainly can't access our intuition in all that chaos, and we become increasingly anxious, unsatisfied and unhappy. We need an intervention — a circuit breaker — to investigate these fear programs below deck. The beauty of this is that the intervention is also the thing that increases our intuition. And what is that intervention? It is making friends with those fear impulses rather than hiding from them.

For example, a friend asks us out for coffee. We feel an instant pull away from that idea. Our intuitive knowledge is guiding us to a day of rest and solitude. Instead of stating our needs, 'I need to be alone today and meditate', we guess at our friend's response. We don't want them to feel rejected. We don't want to get into a confrontation with our friend. Ultimately, we don't want our friend to withdraw their approval of us. We may have been taught consistently from the beginning of our lives that being 'good' and compliant is more important than honouring our instincts. Attending to other people's needs is more appropriate than acknowledging our own. We have most definitely learnt from our early relationships that approval will be withdrawn if we do not do what is expected of us.

As we weigh up the consequences of telling our friend we don't want to accept their invitation, all of this early programming is running beneath the surface in our subconscious. When we finally decide one way or the other, it will respond to that fear program.

Without the circuit breaker of curious and creative self-investigation of the fearful thought, we will be in reactive mode. We will either betray ourselves by accepting the invitation. Or we will lie to our friend and make up an excuse for not going and then guiltily hide at home. With the circuit breaker, we receive the invitation. We feel the contraction caused by the subconscious fear,

*I won't be approved of,*

and we get curious. We are not necessarily even close to a conscious connection to that subconscious fear program. But we are aware of the discomfort, and we are willing to go deeper into it rather than run from it. This is the first and most crucial step. We're no longer on the run from ourselves.

Then we're in flow with life. We are not in a fear-dominant state. When psychological fear rises, we can be curious, open and willing to know more. We say,

*Right, my intuition wants to talk to me, and perhaps I've just not been listening because I was afraid. But here I am now.*

When my students have a fear impulse come up from their subconscious, they now say,

*Awesome, let's do this. I have an opportunity to get to know myself better.*

The fundamental question now is, how do we do this?

# We use fear to clear fear

We must stop avoiding our fear because avoidance of fear is where we develop addiction and numb ourselves to our intuitive knowing. When we think of fear as a problem, we will do whatever we can to avoid our fear. When we think of fear as a friendly ally, we get curious. We say,

*I'm ready. I'm going to sit down. I'm going to stop everything I'm doing, and I'm going to spend five minutes investigating this friendly fear to bring me back to my truth.*

We suddenly diffuse all the bombs that could potentially otherwise go off in the brain and ricochet into reactive choices in our lives.

Let's walk through the process (find the link to the guided journey at the end of this chapter).

**Step one.** I'm sitting here in my office, everything's fine. I'm working away, doing my thing, and suddenly I get hit by anxiety. I'm like,

*Ooh, hello? I suddenly feel really anxious. I don't know what this means, but here's what I'm going to do. I'm going to get curious.*

What I used to do was just keep ploughing on. I would ignore the feeling and have another cup of coffee. I used to say (subconsciously),

*I don't feel comfortable with this feeling, maybe I'll have a drink to numb myself out, or I'll buy something on the internet I don't need to get a temporary dopamine hit, or maybe I'll pick a fight with my partner to drown out this feeling with more chaos and make it someone else's problem.*

But that's the old me.

**Step two.** Instead, I go into the state of being that allows me to get curious. I turn off my phone. Shut my door. Create some quiet.

I sit in this space, and I observe myself. I can feel this anxiety. It feels like a nine out of ten in intensity, ten being the most intense, and that's not comfortable. Nothing fearful has come up today that I am aware of; I'm not expecting any trouble; I haven't had any email telling me bad things are happening. I'll just sit here holding my curiosity around this feeling of anxiety that I rate at a nine because I know I am not in danger.

**Step three.** Now I am ready to move out of my Reasoning Conscious Mind and into my heart's Intuitive Intelligence, knowing that the most profound intuition resides in my heart. I close my eyes. I deepen my breath. I sigh out my breath the first three times to stimulate my vagus nerve (more on that in Chapter Eight) and regulate my nervous system. Then I let my breathing return to its natural rhythm. I place two fingers at the centre of my chest. I imagine my breath moving in and out of my heart space. I do this until I feel anchored in my heart.

**Step four.** I simply ask the question,

*What's beneath this feeling of anxiety?*

I let my deep intuitive knowledge show me the answer. I might feel, hear, see or know the deeper meaning. Fear of abandonment, rejection, lack, worthiness, just to name a common few. As I come into the sacred chamber of my heart, everything slows down. I can sense where my consciousness has been fixated on the past or projected into the future, creating this anxiety. For example, in the stillness, I recall I have a big meeting coming up, and I'm doing a presentation. This subconscious fear that I will fail is sitting beneath the surface of my reasoning conscious mind.

Rather than bypassing it or ignoring it, I acknowledge it. Ah, fear of failure. That old chestnut. I can recall a hundred incidents of feeling like I have failed in my past. I honour this fear because it is the problem, and it's the solution. It holds the answer within it. I want to sit inside of the answer. I want to sit here because I change the energy wherever I place my intention and attention. Ignoring this fear creates more of it.

**Step Five.** Now I get a choice to change my neurological and physiological response to that fear of failure. I'm going to change that subconscious program. I have tended to it, witnessed it, and brought it into sharp focus. I am aware now of what created the anxiety. But self-awareness is not enough. Knowing why I have this fear is not the endpoint for me. I am more powerful than that.

There are two things I can do now in this process. One is I can move into a feeling of gratitude for the fear showing up to let me know where I have forgotten my infinite truth. I can sit with gratitude for that fear of failure and just whisper to it, like a precious part of me,

*Thank you. Thank you for showing me where I have a faulty fear belief running beneath the surface, which, if I leave unchecked, is going to dominate all of my life. Thank you for bringing this up to my attention so that I can process it and release it.*

Rather than it being stored in my biology and coming up, again and again, every time something challenges me and makes me feel a potential fear of the future for whatever reason, I'm going to just be here with my fear. I'm just going to honour it and say,

*Yeah, I get it. I get it. I understand. My history has shown me that this fear is potentially going to be realised. I may have judged that I failed before, but today I'm just present with this fear, and I'm just feeling deep gratitude that it had the courage to show up and to show me and to give me some insight into the truth of who and what I am.*

Now, the second option I have here when I've been doing this practice for a while, and I should be doing it daily, is to move straight into a feeling of gratitude. This advanced practice doesn't require me to engage in mental activity. I'm not looking to find something to be grateful for outside of me because, through consistent use of this practice, I've trained myself to be able to hold that high vibration at will.

Via either approach, I am changing my vibrational frequency at will. I am aware that I can train my consciousness to move frequency at will, without any external change occurring. My boss doesn't need to call me to tell me they know I'll do a great job. I don't have to worry about my presentation obsessively. I am simply changing my subconscious belief that I will fail because I have judged myself as having failed before by holding my attention on a higher frequency.

**Step six.** I melt into this high vibrational feeling state for around 2-3 minutes, lovingly bringing my attention back to the feeling when my mind wanders. After a while of self-exploration with this practice, I might know that music, movement, nature, chanting, toning, or any manner of things supports me to access the highest vibrational state with the most ease.

**Step seven.** When I feel to, I let the feeling go and lower my hand to my lap. I take a deep breath in through the nose and out through the mouth with a sigh. Then I look around for the initial feeling of anxiety that I rated at nine, and I notice what level on a scale of one to ten that I'm feeling now.

I notice the number is two, and I'm good. That is the end of the practice for me.

So what have I just done? Fear arose. I chose to meet it consciously. I changed my physiological response. I trained myself away from that dysregulated addiction to that stressful, anxiety-ridden feeling and created a whole new reality.

If the number were above two, I would go back into that high vibrational feeling, either through the mental activity or not, do that for another minute or two, and then come out and rate it again.

I would do that up to three times. After that, there's a good chance that if I haven't brought the number down, I haven't hit on the deepest layer of the fear. What I mean by that is when I went in and inquired,

*What's beneath this feeling of anxiety?*

I felt fear of failure. But it might be that that is my go-to answer. Maybe fear of failure is something I get all the time, and so I'm like,

*Yeah, it's fear of failure.*

But when I feel into it, there is something more profound — something stickier and meaner, and I don't necessarily like it. But I'm humbly curious, and I'm willing, and I want to be free of this program.

With another fully conscious breath, I notice that beneath the fear of failure is a fear of abandonment.

*If I fail, I will be abandoned. I will be alone.*

Then I take myself into gratitude for that fear.

That's the process of loving, curious investigation of my subconscious fear. I call it the Micro Method, as it is a mini version of a longer process that my students master to serve others.

We often think of fear as just those big, scary emotional states, but fear is anything that is not bliss. Because bliss is the baseline, we should be expecting bliss as our daily norm, and we've taught ourselves to live in a much less joyful state. Fear rising in the body as an impulse of our intuition might appear as anxiety, stress, addiction, depression, anger, frustration, jealousy, irritability, resentment, sadness, rage or grief.

All of these states of being are a form of fear. Remember, fear is not the problem. We're not trying to avoid the fear. Fear is there for us to understand something. It's,

*Knock, knock, knock. Hey, you've forgotten something about yourself. Let's guide you back to that truth.*

Don't think of fear as just the big tsunamis of traumatic events, but even the smallest twinge. This is my favourite example. I walk into the bathroom. My partner has left their clothes on the floor *next to* the laundry basket yet again. In the bedroom, the wet towel is on the bed. In my body, there's that twinge of urgh! I'm not going to go and have a full-blown argument with my partner (not today anyway), but I am aware that I am not in a place of joy right now. Life is not feeling joyful. Rather than ignoring the feeling, I will be curious about it. I discovered through the Micro Method that I have a fear of rejection. If I ask for what I need, my subconscious fear is that my partner will reject me. I do the work, not just once, not just this day, but every time I feel that frustration and neutralise the fear program.

The upshot of this is that I can then speak from my heart to my partner about what I need to thrive — a clean bedroom, an even share of domestic labour, and respect for my personal space. This process has nothing to do with accepting behaviour from others that is not acceptable but neutralising the subconscious program. When I do this often enough, my external reality will become congruent with my new and improved self-belief.

The key to success with this is absolutely the earlier we jump onto that slightly not full of bliss thought or feeling, the quicker that we're going to be able to find ease in all parts of our lives in relation to fear. The more we train ourselves to be curious about the times that fear rises in the little ways, the less likely we're going to have those tsunamis of emotions. We have become self-reliant and self-regulating. We are no longer externalising our power. Now, instead of saying that,

*I feel anxious because the planets are misaligned or because he's a Scorpio, or I forgot to charge my crystals in the full moon,*

I create a new reality. Fear is a friendly ally. Fear is serving us as a form of our intuition.

Please understand that this is a new way of being for most of us. Like all good things, it takes practice, practice, practice. The more we do the Micro Method, the more we can change our neurological response, shift that dominant subconscious fear program, and move quickly into a higher frequency.

## Discomfort

Our biggest problem with increasing our intuition is we're mostly trying to avoid discomfort. We simply need to see fear as a friendly ally guiding us home to the truth of what we are. Our intuition is off the charts because there's no separation between us and the Superconscious Mind when we do that.

I recall a student listening to all of this in class one day. She asked me with genuine concern on her face,

*Can you confuse your flow state as really just a state which is comfortable?*

Yes! I exclaimed. She'd identified a key issue on the path of embodying Intuitive Intelligence. A dysregulated nervous system can become very addicted to the comfort zone. That's why it's essential we talk about discomfort not being a problem but expected on this journey. When I say flow, I don't mean the absence of effort. Discomfort usually suggests that our sense of ourselves is disoriented, and disorientation is very powerful because we all cling to the comfort zone. We're comfortable. Life might be working pretty well for us. We might have a lovely partner in a nice house and a couple of kids, and there's no big drama. Yet, our soul is agitating for something bigger. Our soul is saying,

*I want more.*

Our soul is yearning to meet itself at higher and higher levels, and our comfort zone is saying,

*No, I'm good. Just stay here. Do not change anything. Don't rock the boat.*

We should more accurately describe the comfort zone as the *familiar* zone because usually, it is not comfortable at all, but it is well known. That's what the ego is seeking because it controls the known.

Then we follow that agitation without necessarily even knowing why. We do something like sign up for a yoga course or do a juice cleanse or anything that's outside of our routine, and our ego will go into a panic and say,

*You're going to ruin everything. Don't change anything. Stay inside of your comfort zone.*

A few years ago, my friend was telling me about a fantastic job opportunity that included an overseas move. It was something she had been working towards her whole career. It was the job of a lifetime, but as soon as she received the offer, she delayed responding to it for several weeks because she couldn't shake the feeling of worry. Suddenly, this amazing opportunity seemed all wrong. I met up with her a few months later and asked her what she had decided to do. She had turned the offer down. It just didn't feel right. As soon as she did, she felt relieved. Her current situation wasn't that bad, and, she added, at least she knew what she was getting.

On the surface, this might look like my friend had followed her intuition on the surface. But that isn't the case. She had instead followed the voice of her ego. Her whole career, she had worked up to this moment, and when it arrived, she was terrified of the unknown and the change the move would bring. It was way beyond her comfort/familiar zone. So, she did what we so often do. She lied to herself. She let herself believe that it wasn't really what she wanted. She didn't expand into the growth zone. As a result, she soothed her ego and got an immediate sense of relief.

We often say things like,

*Oh, my intuition let me down because this bad thing happened.*

*SOMETHING WENT WRONG when I listened to my intuition. Something went wrong, so my intuition must be faulty.*

*I can't tell the difference between my intuition and my fear.*

*I just don't know what my intuition is saying.*

These illusions are usually a defence of the ego to keep us in a known state of being.

Intuitive Intelligence is taking us away from illusion and into truth. Our ego identified personality often does not want the truth because where our intuition will lead us is inevitably into growth and expansion. Our intuition is the language of consciousness, so as we raise consciousness, we leave more and more of the known world, the comfort/familiar zone behind us, and we move more into the learning zone.

Our ego gets very uncomfortable with that. So we pretend to ourselves. We are playing this game with ourselves. We're hiding from the truth of what our intuition is guiding us to. Instead of doing what we thought our intuition was meant to do, which was to help us avoid any discomfort and always stay in this nice, familiar life, intuition leads us into a space of superconsciousness.

If we think we open to our intuition so that we can avoid bad things ever happening to us, then we've missed the point because those bad things are only bad, according to our judgement of them. We assess based on our prior history and an imaginary future. Some things will happen to us that we would prefer not to happen, but it isn't a problem unless we judge it.

Our intuition, like our spirituality, is not designed to stop us from suffering but rather to help us navigate that suffering journey from a higher perspective because intuition opens us to our symbolic sight. We're able to see the deeper meaning of our life events because of our Intuitive Intelligence, rather than using intuition to attempt to avoid ever suffering.

One of the things that we must learn to do is sit with the discomfort that our intuition will often guide us to. Things get uncomfortable because the truth is rising, consciousness is increasing, and that is the very point of our lives, and we're like,

*Oh, this discomfort, I don't want this discomfort. It means something's gone wrong.*

And we are looking to avoid rather than to expand. My invitation is to go directly into those feelings of discomfort.

## Superconscious Sight

Meeting our subconscious fear is ultimately a willingness to get over our littleness and to see ourselves and the world with *spiritual sight*. It is a return to our wholeness/holiness. *A Course in Miracles* tells us that there is nothing to fear[16]. It is impossible even to understand this when we look at the world with human sight. We cannot solve our life situations, our issues or meet our fears at the level at which they are created. It is simply not possible. Spiritual sight begins when we are willing to surrender to that greater part of ourselves. We

---

16 *A Course in Miracles*, | W-48.1:1-5. Accessed: https://acim.org/acim/en/s/450#1:1-5 | W-48.1:1-5

acknowledge that something greater than our limited human consciousness guides our lives.

Even when we do not understand the events of our life, we do not doubt them. It is a state of being that requires deep trust in the infinite intelligence of the Cosmos, and it is the most powerful creative power we possess. Living beyond our fear liberates our creative vision and allows us to align with what we are truly meant to express in the world. Another way to think about this is that the unique mission that God has for us is set free, and we follow the path that inevitably unfolds with ease and grace because we know we are not alone. This is spiritual sight — to look at the events of our lives with absolute trust.

Our unwillingness to engage with our fear prevents us from embodying our holiness/wholeness. Our unlimited consciousness is just on the other side of fear. That is power. It's such a power that many of us never allow ourselves into that state of questioning. We never question our beliefs, so we prevent ourselves from ever taking responsibility for our own lives. Our fear causes us to be more in this dense state of form, so, on a quantum level, fear is slowing us down. We can come into such a dense state that we are incapable of knowing our infinite nature. When we consciously start working with our intuition, we break through that dense state.

We are breaking free. When we are free, we are faster, and we are lighter. When we meet our fear and emancipate ourselves from it, we lighten our load and raise ourselves up from our dominant physical reality that is ruled by our five senses. In this state, fear becomes a friendly ally. It shows us where we have left the path of fearlessness so we can return and no longer be vulnerable to that particular fear.

The greatest power I have is to change my mind about what I am. That also means we change our minds about what the world is. I have the power to change the world that I see by changing my mind about what I am. My perception is everything. When I change to spiritual sight or spiritual perception, I am no longer at war with the world. I no longer judge anything as good or bad. It simply is and what it is, is an opportunity for me to accept that I am God.

What would it take for us to live without judgement of good or bad and surrender to radical acceptance? To know that everything that we see is serving us. The next step, of course, is that everything we see we have created as a way to awaken. That is what our consciousness does. If we want to awaken through joy, that is our choice right now. We make that choice to change our minds about the world and what we are. Any suffering is self-imposed.

I'll say that again because that may feel like I'm accusing us all of creating our misery, and I guess I have to say I am. Any suffering is self-imposed. There are no circumstances that are excluded from this. But what happens when we accept this with love rather than a sense of weight, or as though we're punished because we haven't made good choices, is that what we see will change because we're no longer at war with the world.

We hear that there is a kind of circular logic here. We cannot see something different until we're willing to change our minds about what we're currently seeing. We have no greater power than to change our minds about what we're seeing. For that is where we become a true creative power. Spiritual sight is the only true sight. Our human sight, our belief that things have gone wrong, that there is good and bad, that we are either being punished or rewarded by God, is a nightmare. It is a freakish vision. It has nothing to do with reality. Reality is living in accordance with the law. Reality is accepting that heaven on earth is now if we are willing to change our minds.

We're talking to all of the laws here because the laws are always the key back to the truth. The fastest way for us to remind ourselves when we have fallen into the habit of thinking like a human is to ask ourselves the question,

*Am I living in accordance with the law? Am I holding a low fearful vibration and expecting to see a joyful world?*

It's simply not possible. The law of correspondence tells me this because these two opposing beliefs cannot correspond. They cannot communicate with one another.

*Do I believe that changing the world happens at the level of form and matter? Or am I reminding myself of the law of mentalism that all is of the mind?*

If we want to see a different reality, we must change our minds about the reality we're seeing.

## Spiritual Self-Esteem

When we come back to the correction of perception, again and again, we live with spiritual self-esteem. Spiritual self-esteem is not like ordinary self-esteem. It is the sense of self that comes from power combined with humility. Power plus humility ensures that we live with spiritual sight and inhabit our spiritual self-esteem. The gospel of St. John tells us this, 'I can of my own self do nothing.[17]' Here we go further into the paradox of

---

17 John 5:30 KJV

spiritual sight. I am everything, and I am nothing — what a relief.

When we understand that all we need to do is surrender back into our infinite nature, we surrender to God every time we try to control the outcome. We fall back into the embrace of the infinite that is always there. We let go of believing that we need to have power over something to know our truth. The world is built on that faulty foundation. The world is built on the idea that power is power *over* something else. That I have climbed the ladder higher than someone below me means that I am more powerful.

This has nothing to do with true power. The true power of God or the true power of Intuitive Intelligence is wholeness/holiness. The symbol of this is a circle. Within it, all is contained. Nothing is excluded, and everything within it has the same power level all at once.

An intuition without the self-esteem to act upon it is simply yet another trinket and superstition. We might as well go and buy those Oracle cards and not take action unless we get the right Oracle card on the right day under the right phase of the moon.

All of that is the externalisation of our power, and it has no place here. The truth is this. We are overcoming the belief in separation so that we may return (although only in our minds because we never left in truth) to our rightful place in that infinite, expansive consciousness that everything is made of. Spiritual self-esteem is the self-worth to let the God voice lead.

Don't be afraid of true power, which will invite us to withdraw all need for approval from the world.

*Am I good with God?*

We will be less than our true holy power until this question is our guide. Why? Because the world has been sold a lie about the nature of spiritual truth. It is not about finding a comfortable little corner of the world and tuning out. It is about tuning in and getting as uncomfortable as hell in order to walk the path of awakening. Forgo our comfort and the need to make others comfortable, and we'll meet our evolution. This is spiritual fierceness. This is spiritual self-esteem, and it takes time to emerge.

Our task is not to keep the world happy and approve of us. Our greatest freedom is to become self-reliant. If we look outside of ourselves for approval, we will inevitably compromise ourselves. This does not mean that we don't reflect and review our actions. It doesn't mean we lack humility or remain ignorant to our shadow behaviours. It means we can listen to others' opinions without immediate emotional reaction. We are willing to evolve *and* aware of our worth just as we are. The two things are not mutually exclusive. This is humility. This is the seat of self-approval.

**Resources**

Find the guided Micro-Method here:
https://instituteforintuitiveintelligence.com/si-resources/

# PART TWO:
# THE EVOLUTION

*Dear God,*
*In humility, I stand before the sacred chamber of my heart.*
*I am requesting permission to enter ever more deeply.*
*I recognise my desire to hold myself back*
*from fully merging with the power of my holiness.*
*Today, I surrender to myself.*
*This surrender alters me*
*and i am made more holy by it.*
*Refine me.*
*Make me in your image.*
*Let your grace dance in my soul and on my tongue.*
*And so it is.*
*And it is so.*

# Chapter 5

# The Phases of Intuition Maturity

*"Intuition is tied to acceptance. When we can free ourselves from the need to control the outcomes of situations in life, accepting that there is a wisdom and a greater reason for everything, we open ourselves to be guided by the signs of the universe through intuition."*

—*Sri Prem Baba.*

The two broad categories of intuition help us understand the level of consciousness we access when utilising them. Local intuition, which includes being empathic and highly sensitive, pertains to the local dimension. As we have come to understand, nonlocal intuition functions because of the inherent interconnectedness of all consciousness. The immutable laws explain it. Within these two broad categories are four phases of intuition that also map our consciousness.

As we have explored nonlocal intuition so fully in the science chapter, I want to share a little more on local intuition to support our investigation of the four phases. Our local intuition is biological and informed by our electrical-magnetic composition. We are electromagnetic beings who produce energetic fields. We are sensitive to one another's energy and the energy of everything around us. Energetic sensitivity refers to the 'ability of our body and nervous system to detect electromagnetic and other types of energetic signals in the environment[18]' according to the HeartMath Institute. People who identify as empathic or highly sensitive (also known as empaths) fall into this biological intuition category.

We are all empathic and highly sensitive, and when we understand our electromagnetic biology, it becomes clear why. We are constantly collecting energetic information from one another, most often without realising it. When we live in the Intuitive Intelligence embodied state, there are powerful ways that this energetic sensitivity can be part of our toolkit for living in extraordinary times. Rather than being something that makes us too sensitive to inhabit the world, we begin to understand the information provided to us through this kind of intuition and how to use it to our advantage.

The other reason why this is important is that we may be inadvertently stunting our spiritual evolution by thinking that being able to feel information in someone's energy field while in proximity to them is our highest form of intuition. That is only one kind of intuition. I recently attended a women's circle, and we were invited to introduce ourselves to the group. One of the women introduced herself as a *true empath*. I could only assume that she meant she was 'more' empathic than the rest of us or that she was different to all others who describe themselves in this way. I came to discover that, according to her assessment, she suffers more. She explained how weary and

18 Accessed at: https://www.heartmath.org/research/science-of-the-heart/energetic-communication/

overwhelmed she was because she is so sensitive to everyone's energy and world events. This was just her lot, her burden to carry because of her affliction/gift of being a 'true empath'. I could tell she was genuinely convinced of all that she shared. And that she had no intention of changing anything. I mean by this that she was certain that this was the height of spirituality. She was born this way; she'd stay this way. Her work was as an energy healer. I suppose it served her to stay at this level of belief. But how much richer and more rewarding, and less *exhausting* her life would be if she asked,

*What else is possible? Is it God's flawed design that the more spiritual I am, the less I am able to thrive in the world?*

Local intuition is one aspect of a much larger power. It is my great hope that we do not resist our intuition evolution by clinging to the known.

As we look at this map, I would also like us to be aware that we never do away with any of our forms of intuition. We're not trying to evolve beyond them. But we are trying to mature them. All four phases — primary, reactive, communion, and surrender — will remain with us throughout the entirety of our lived experience. But as we mature and attain more spiritual agency and become less reactive to the world, the more we're able to see the evidence of this. This is why I see intuition as a map of consciousness. The ultimate goal is not to increase intuition. It's consciousness-raising that we seek.

# THE FOUR PHASES OF INTUITION

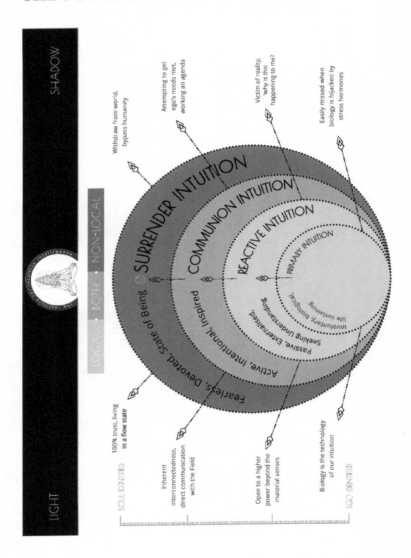

There are four kinds of intuition within the two broad categories of nonlocal and local, and each has a shadow and light form. The four phases are primary, reactive, communion and surrender. Primary intuition and reactive intuition both fall into the local category of intuition. Communion intuition is both local and nonlocal intuition. The final phase, Surrender intuition, is entirely nonlocal.

The diagram shows that these circles get larger as we move out. We're demonstrating that when we get to the final phase of intuition, all the other phases of intuition are contained within. We are never without all four phases of our intuition, but we evolve through them. The function of this map is to help us understand where we are in our relationship with our intuition.

We can think about the journey from primary intuition, a purely biological state, to surrender intuition which is strictly a nonlocal, non-biological state, as a measure or map of our consciousness-raising. Intuition is a secondary benefit of raising our consciousness. The more we keep increasing our intuition, the more we raise our spiritual awareness. If we keep working with our intuition, we will inevitably awaken to our Superconsciousness at greater and greater levels.

As discussed throughout this book, we understand the nature of intuition by understanding the relationships between dimensions. The nonlocal dimension (pure energy, pure consciousness, superconsciousness) informs the local (matter, body, Conscious Reasoning Mind) through the fourth dimension (subtle anatomy, subconscious Mind). The fourth dimension is intuition, imagination, inspiration, language, feeling — intangible elements. We can understand that intuition is a form of communication between the Superconscious Mind and us, which contains all time and space. It is the bridge between pure energy and matter, or superconsciousness and the Conscious Reasoning Mind.

This map is not simply the phases of intuition; we are mapping the stages of our spiritual evolution. We can think of this in terms of spiritual agency. This is a measure of our relationship to our spiritual power, for agency means power. How much agency a person has, indicates how much power they have in their own life. In this diagram, the more superconsciousness-identified we are, the more spiritual agency we possess. We can also think of this in terms of the amount of subconscious fear we are holding. The more we move towards surrender intuition, the less fear we carry.

We also consider the shadow and light aspects of each phase. We can naively assume that intuition, in all ways, is positive. This can stem from the belief that intuition is a gift that only some possess. Intuition is not a gift. It is a fact. All things can be utilised for good or bad, shadow or light. For our purposes, the consideration of shadow and light points us to how we may be misusing or abusing our personal power. For example,

*Where might I be utilising my intuition to manipulate and control versus gaining deeper surrender to divine will?*

For most of us, abuses and misuses occur because we have not been taught about intuition and have not been encouraged to train it. The discussion of shadow and light relates very well to our understanding of fear and what happens to our consciousness when we have unmet subconscious fear stored in our bodies.

By understanding the intuitions within intuition, we are equipped to have a more sophisticated conversation about intuition and to increase our access to our highest form of intelligence. Intuition is far more nuanced and multi-faceted than we are led to believe, and this is why so many never mature beyond the rudimentary levels. This knowledge equips us to do better. Let's explore each of the phases now.

# Primary intuition

**Qualities: Passive, local, involuntary, unconscious, shallow, very little agency, non-participatory**

We begin by understanding a rudimentary survival intuition, also known as gut instinct, which I refer to as primary intuition.

Primary intuition pertains to our capacity to tune into the electromagnetic frequencies of those around us, which is our biology. There's nothing spiritual or nonlocal about that. We're picking up information from each other and the local field all of the time. This is because of the makeup of our biology. We're picking up information unconsciously through the interaction of our fields. It's the kind of intuition that's most often written about and discussed. When articles get documented and popularised in the media, they generally reference this form of intuition. Yet it's a primitive, basic instinct. It is 100% necessary for our survival, and we don't want to be without it. But we also don't want to stop here.

Primary intuition is unconscious. We don't choose when or how it shows up. Like breathing, it is a function of the autonomic nervous system. It happens involuntarily, although as we've seen, we can numb ourselves to it as we have learnt in the anatomy of fear. It doesn't require our participation or conscious commitment to developing it.

Primary intuition alerts us to when we are in danger, not because we can see a threat in our environment, but because we can sense it through the information shared through the field of our environment and those within it. For example, when we walk through our neighbourhood, we just know not to go down a particular street that day. We've taken that familiar route every other day, but today it feels off. Or when we are in our car and want to turn right at that intersection to get to work, we feel like going left today. Or we meet someone for the first time, and we are sure that they are not a good person, even though nothing in their appearance indicates so. We have evolved to detect threats in our environment to survive. So how can this ever be a negative?

There are several ways we can be in our shadow with our primary intuition. Very often, this is where we stop in terms of our evolution. Even at this level, we are suspicious of it. We consider it spiritual or outrageous or *out there.* The idea that we would trust something other than our minds to discern whether a decision is right or wrong seems to be so antithetical to the world that we shut that down. So we ignore it. We override ourselves. In doing so, we end up in situations that go against life. We ignore ourselves and inadvertently put ourselves in harm's way.

We can also shut it down through dysregulation of our nervous system, where we will become so addicted to living in the stress hormones of fight or flight that we can't discern what our gut is saying. We're stuck in a cycle where we think it's our intuition, and it's just our dysregulation creating stress hormones. That means we keep misidentifying what our intuition is and making poor choices.

Until we learn to break the addiction to living in that fight-or-flight response, until we learn how to regulate our nervous system, our biological form of intuition can be very, very off.

We can't trust that internal GPS when we're in that addiction through the dysregulated nervous system. Our most basic biological form of intuition is being skewed or prevented from operating properly because a more dominant program runs: addiction to living in a dysregulated state of being. We may become a stranger to ourselves, and we make choices that go against life, that go against our very survival.

**A note on rewilding**

Yet another shadow aspect of this phase of intuition is how we are domesticated out of receiving it properly. We are born with a very healthy primary intuition. We have a wild, intuitive knowing.

Then, as many of us experienced, we are taught to be polite and good, fit in at the café, be nice to grandpa, or sit on that man's lap that we don't like, and just behave ourselves. We educate our children out of connection to primary intuition, that primal wild knowing. When a child is resistant to hug a person, for example, but the mother insists they must do so the mother fears disapproval. She is afraid of being judged as a bad parent who has raised a disobedient child. She feels embarrassed that her child is not following her instruction. The mother is feeling all of this because she was raised this way. So she forces her child to ignore the child's primary intuition, and the child learns she cannot trust her feelings, continuing the cycle.

We mature into adults who don't have a clue because we have been taught to distrust ourselves and privilege being polite and good as our highest value over honouring our primary intuition. This is even more if we are raised in environments including education systems that are dangerous to us, either emotionally, physically, mentally, or all of the above. We learned how to contract and shut ourselves down to survive. The child knows this is an unsafe environment. But if they try to advocate for themselves, they will often be taught that they are naughty and might be severely punished for that.

We have a choice here about rewilding ourselves as the first act of connecting back to primary intuition and then raising our children and our grandchildren differently.

When our child says,

*No. I don't want to go to swimming class today. I do not need another extracurricular activity. I just need to go and dig in the dirt in the back garden,*

We simply say,

*Okay, child. Go be with that. Because that is what your wild intuitive knowing is telling you. And that's how I keep you trusting yourself.*

The biggest issue with our intuition is that we don't trust it because we have been taught not to trust ourselves.

The light form of primary intuition begins our connection to something greater than discerning through the conscious reasoning mind's five senses. Even though it's our most basic form of intuition, it doesn't mean we don't want it. It is our protective field. It opens us and activates us to our more subtle forms of communication. It's the foundation of self-trust, the precursor to any healthy relationship with intuition.

I want to share a remarkable experience of primary intuition from my own life with you. It is the story of the birth of my first child. I was 42 weeks when I was admitted for labour to be induced. After several hours and no effect from the gel applied to my cervix designed to get labour going, the young doctor said she wanted to break my waters. I had read everything. I knew that the hospital protocol was to try the gel one more time before this next step she was now recommending. I was uncertain, but also so keen to meet my baby. I didn't question her.

I vividly recall the wash of amniotic fluid rushing around me on the bed as the young doctor broke my waters.

*So much fluid for a baby who is two weeks overdue.*

The doctor looked up at me with something akin to terror in her eyes. It was not what I wanted to see. The midwife in the room exchanged some terse words with the young doctor, still hovering between my legs. All I remember hearing was *cord prolapse.* I knew what that meant. Like many first-time mothers, I had spent my pregnancy reading everything I could on being pregnant and what could go wrong. Umbilical cord prolapse is a complication that occurs before or during the baby's delivery. The umbilical cord drops (prolapses) through the open cervix into the vagina ahead of the baby in a prolapse. The cord can then become trapped against the baby's body during delivery. It results in a lack of oxygen for the baby. The consequences of that don't need to be spelt out. The resulting action is called a crash caesar in medical jargon – the most emergency of all emergency caesars. In other words,

*get the baby out immediately.*

Someone hit the button on the wall or made the call. The emergency was declared on the speakers throughout the hospital. Within moments medical staff choked the small room. I knew I was supposed to get onto my hands and knees to take pressure off the cord and to free up the oxygen supply to my unborn baby. Someone got me into this position, a doctor on the gurney behind me, pushing the head away from the cord. Within minutes I was several floors up in the hospital operating theatre looking into the face of the anaesthetist as he counted down from ten. The last thing I heard was a doctor yelling,

*we have to get this baby out of her.*

Then everything went black. My firstborn son was brought into the world seven minutes after my waters were broken. They tell me he cried out straight away and has been a strong, healthy boy (now nearly a man) ever since. I share this story as evidence of primary intuition at work. I never went into labour. I never even had one contraction. I was in a tertiary hospital when the emergency occurred. Had I gone into labour at home, as is the norm for most mothers, it is unlikely that my son would have survived.

How did my body know not to kick off the chemical and hormonal changes that establish labour? How did my baby know to stay put? To me, this is the most beautiful proof of the unconscious phase of our intuition at work.

## Reactive intuition

**Qualities: Local, passive, biological, intermittent, conscious, shallow, minimal spiritual agency, non-participatory**

Reactive intuition is when we are willing to believe that intuition *is out there in the world*, but we don't yet believe it is within us, at least not in any consistent or beneficial way. We will seek someone, or something we think has access to that intuitive information. We do not yet believe that we have access to that information. We think intuition is a gift, and only some people have it.

When we are in a state of crisis or confusion, we will seek out the psychic, or the tarot reader or the healer, who will help us believe that there's some bigger picture, there's some relief. There's someone who knows what's going on, even though we have no freaking idea and feel completely out of control. We're reacting and in reactionary mode to the world, desperately on the hunt for something to give us some sense of certainty.

Maybe our husband left, we're in a financial crisis, or we've got a health issue, and we want some answers. We want to believe that someone or something out there can give us some peace of mind and that someone else can take responsibility for our life for a time. We want someone to answer the questions of our life. It is a spiritually immature relationship with intuition. The idea that intuition is a gift is something that we like to believe because it lets us off the hook of thinking that we have it, and we may need to train it and put the time in to get clear in our access to it. We're not ready for that kind of personal power. We don't even know we have that kind of power at this stage.

I spent years as a shop psychic. It's the best apprenticeship I ever did because I learned so much about this phase of intuition. I had people coming back to me every week asking me to tell them every detail of their life. They wanted to know if their boyfriend was cheating if he was the one, or if they should sell their house or change jobs. They came to me because they were terrified of taking personal responsibility for their choices. They didn't know how to trust themselves because of that broken relationship with their primary intuition. I eventually had to walk away from all of that because I wanted to empower them with their connection to intuition, and they wanted to give me their power. But I'm so grateful for it because it taught me to understand how we begin to connect to intuition. I understood that we are afraid of the world and our own lives.

In this phase, we often feel like a victim of reality. We'll cry,

*Why is this happening to me?*

Rather than reflecting on our behaviour and taking personal responsibility,

*Okay, my husband left me because I was engaging in childish behaviour. I was spending money like a fool; I wasn't taking responsibility for anything. What's my part in this breakup?*

Instead of doing that, we are looking at the world as though we are the victim of it. We don't want to know, and we don't want to take personal responsibility. Tuning into and training our intuition for ourselves would no longer permit us to stay in the victim role.

We understand that there are no watchers in the quantum field from quantum physics. We are never passively receiving life. We are always making choices, and we don't necessarily acknowledge that we are making those choices, so it feels as if life happens to us. We say,

*I don't know how this chaos happened.*

*I don't know how I'm in another shitty relationship.*

*I don't know how I'm in debt again.*

*I don't know how I'm in a job I hate.*

We believe that intuition will hold the answer to the perfect person, job, place to live and so on, as though these things exist somewhere and we haven't found them yet. We are passive recipients of our lives, mainly because we have not been shown other possibilities. For some of us, the frustration of ricocheting from one crisis to the next activates our awakening consciousness. This space invites us to become *intuition-curious*. We say,

*I could buy a crystal that might increase my intuition or an oracle deck to give me some answers. And I'm willing to try. I'm willing to try to imagine that there is a possibility that knowledge and information out there will help ease the burden of this human experience.*

When we're in the light form, it is the gateway to higher and higher states of spiritual agency. Reactive intuition is the opening to the belief in a higher power beyond the material senses. It's the beginning of that recognition that the Universe constitutes more than just what is perceived through our five senses. We might start to see signs like 11 or feathers or butterflies, and we feel a higher power is guiding us.

We don't want to dismiss this phase because it is part of our spiritual maturing. We are stepping into that evolution of our consciousness. But it is only a phase, yet so many of us get stuck here. We get stuck in a shadow form that I call spiritual retail therapy. We buy every crystal, dream catcher, and pretty thing from the spiritual shop and every oracle deck. Every single spiritual shop we see, we are in there. It's like shopping but spiritual, and we need it to feel a sense of connection to something greater than ourselves. We want to wear the things that make us feel spiritual. We want to have all those things on us because we know something is happening there. We just don't recognise the truth of it yet. To take that personal responsibility to discover it within us, we need to stop looking outside. How do we do that if no one ever told us that,

*Actually, it's in you too.*

It's okay for us to have those days where we're like,

*I'm just going to keep spinning my pendulum until I get the answer I want.*

Because we don't want the answer, we just want the relief of the burden of the responsibility. The same goes for visiting healers. We often don't want to figure out how to become the energetic healing we need. We want to sit in the field of someone else who makes us feel temporarily better. Then we go home, and we don't make any of the choices we need to make to create the conditions for healing in our lives because that would take a level of personal responsibility that we'd prefer not to invest in. Not because we're wrong, not because we've failed at something. But because A, no one ever told us it's possible. Or B, life is already tremendous, heavy, and overwhelming.

But for most of us, this is the point where we go,

*I want to do that intuition thing for myself.*

We sign up for the tarot course. We go to the Reiki training. We buy all the crystals. We invoke parking angels. Whatever it is, we do decide that actually, maybe it is in me. That's where it starts to get good. That's where we begin to get into active participation with our intuition.

## Communion intuition

**Qualities: Nonlocal and local, active, high level of spiritual agency, deep and shallow states, participatory, conscious and subconscious**

Communion intuition is the recognition that we're in a conversation with greater power. We recognise that there is inherent interconnectedness. We have realised that if we focus our attention, perhaps through our devotional practices, perhaps through having a great capacity to be mindful or to hold a mental image with clarity, we can start to manufacture a reality.

With a little bit of control, we can start to detect that the communion between us, and this greater power is not a one-way street. Something or someone is listening. We experience the reward of an intentional life if we stay focused on what we desire for long enough. This is where the ideas of vision boards and creating gratitude lists, and holding a clear intention for what we want our lives to look like enters our practice.

We see that things we desire come to pass, and even if they don't come to pass in the way we were expecting, we can see that there's a relationship; there's a conversation going on. Now, all of this sounds good, and it is good. It is also simply a stage of our evolution based on walking between two worlds — the local and the nonlocal. It's a stage of development in our spiritual awakening, and it's a stage of evolution in our intuition. If we pursue our intuition, our awakening journey will continue to expand. We cannot pursue the development of our intuition and not see the development of our spiritual nature.

We discover that with passionately focussed attention and intention upon the outcome of what we want and desire, whether it's the answer, or the opportunity, or the car park, it doesn't matter, that it will come to me with ease and grace. Not all of the time, but we're experiencing it enough that we believe it's possible that if we keep going in this direction, we can develop it.

We're beginning to take responsibility for that spiritual maturity to develop our intuition. Everybody is intuitive, and everybody can also speak French. Yet, not everybody will take the time to learn to speak French.

Our intuition is our absolute birthright, but our capacity and skill are choices we make. How willing am I to train my intuition? If we decide to train it, the rewards will be great. And usually, we do that because we want more intuition, right? We don't realise that what we're doing increases our consciousness simultaneously. We typically go towards intuition because we wish for more intuition to get our ego's needs met.

It is excellent to have communion intuition because we recognise that we're more sophisticated than just primary intuition and realise that we have power, unlike reactive intuition. We may not understand the nature of that power, and we don't at this stage, but we're getting closer. We recognise that we can use our mind (and our feeling states when we get a bit more sophisticated) to cultivate a life we want to live.

This is when we recognise consciousness creates itself. When we understand this, we have to accept that fortune telling, energy forecasting, future predictions and consulting oracle cards and signs in all their forms are an act of self-fulfilling prophecy. In truth, all that is happening is that the prediction is collapsing the wave function and drawing down that potential from all the trillions of possibilities to make it so. Depending on how much value we place in the predictor, the more likely we are to build our reality in accordance with that prediction. We create the signs that we are seeking. That is the power when we acknowledge it, and until then, it is a way to lose power.

This understanding happens when we stop using our intuition to rob others of their own power. Just as I had to walk away from being a shop psychic because my clients wanted me to guarantee them a future, we must walk away from believing that we have any right to 'predict' or shape the lives of others with our intuition. The only way we should work with intuition with others is to support them to increase their own access to it. We may unconsciously abuse spiritual agency in this phase because we believe if we 'receive' something about someone else, then we must share it with them. Adyashanti, an American born spiritual teacher, speaks to this in his text, *The End of Your World*, and it is worth quoting here:

*Part of you may find it unpleasant to feel what's happening with people, but another part of you might like it. It's like eavesdropping on someone's energetic state. If we unconsciously find that pleasurable, then it will happen more and more. If, on the other hand, we're not actually that interested — we're not pushing it away, but we're not seeking it out, either — then our attention goes where it is appropriate for it to go. Sometimes it is appropriate to feel what others are feeling, especially if you are in communion or relationship with them; it can help you to understand them in a kinesthetic level. But you start to realize it's not necessary to go around feeling what everybody else is feeling when you're not in relationship with them. You realize their business is their business, not yours[19].*

It is our intention and attention that guides the functioning of our intuition. So if we focus on the energy of others, consciously or unconsciously fixating on being able to 'read' others, then we delay our awakening. This can happen as the ego's attempt to keep us from doing the deep work of awakening consciousness. We become so enamoured of our special skill to intuit for others that we avoid meeting ourselves.

A friend of mine was recently in the unenviable situation of having a sick child with no discernible diagnosis. Doctor

---

19 Adyashanti, *End of Your World*, 2008, p125

after doctor could not identify the reasons for her child's chronic illness, and worse than this, she was often dismissed as a hysterical mother. Sleep deprivation combined with the extreme stress of an ill child left her emotionally vulnerable and physically depleted. She shared some of her experience online with her community, and one day she received a message from an acquaintance. The acquaintance had 'tuned into' my friend, her baby and her partner, and had 'intuitive' information for all of them. She diagnosed the baby as suffering the effects of black mould, even though there was no evidence of this, and she made several sweeping statements about the emotional wellbeing of my friend and her partner.

When my friend shared this with me, suffice to say I was incensed. Not only were these person's assessments incorrect, but they were also unsolicited and, as such, unethical. My friend was tired and vulnerable and easily scared, as she was so desperate to find some relief for her child. This acquaintance's predatory behaviour was not to seek financial remuneration, but she robbed my friend of her personal power. Whether this person knew it or not, that was exactly what she had done. She planted fear in an exhausted mother's mind. My friend was highly suggestible in her depleted state, so her subconscious was easily impressed. The 'intuitive' guidance forced upon my friend caused no good to anyone. In my friend's energetic field without invitation, the uninvited 'reader' was getting off on her power, albeit subconsciously, and collapsing the wave function around an already overwhelming situation. Nothing about what was shared helped to change the situation positively. In all likelihood, the acquaintance was relying on explicit knowledge from what my friend had shared publicly.

So what do I believe should have happened? Rarely should our intuitive knowledge be used to respond to the symptoms of the dream or to access information for another. I train people to support others to increase their own Intuitive Intelligence in my service. We lead people to self-realisation, not realise things for them. It is breaking the law. We often seek intuitive guidance, as we have seen in reactive intuition when we are vulnerable and scared. We are ripe for the picking, desperately seeking answers to alleviate our suffering. It would be ideal if we could instead focus on becoming self-reliant. But we are usually not ready for it at that stage.

Those with clear access to intuition have a far greater moral and ethical responsibility. Once we have established a connection to our Intuitive Intelligence, we must not abuse that power. If we feel we must share something we are intuiting with another, then seek permission. This goes back to the truth that intuition is not special. It is not magical. It is not a requirement for you to share it unsolicited, and when we do, it is usually because we are in the faulty egoic belief that we are special and entitled to dump our 'intuition' on anyone we want.

I describe communion intuition as active, intentional and inspired in its light form. This is where we stop being passive about our relationship to our intuition. We're suddenly aware that we don't need to go to someone else to have that conversation with the Superconscious Mind. We may use very different language, especially at the early phases of communion intuition. We start to get evidence that when we hold our consciousness on an idea for a sustained amount of time, we begin to see reality change. This is very exciting. This is communion. There is a communion occurring between the Superconscious Mind and us. We are beginning to gather evidence that we are not reactive victims of reality. If we show up consistently, we can manufacture or encode our reality. We can begin to direct consciousness. But we are still tuning in and tuning out of intuition. Tune in to ask a question, get some guidance, have a few moments of devotion in the morning or while we're in yoga, and then go back to our normal local reality just wandering through the day, largely oblivious to that higher state of consciousness.

In the light form, this is very exciting because we're aware now that not only are we the agents of our intuition but that there is an inherent interconnectedness between all consciousness and that we are in direct communication with that field.

However, on the shadow side, what happens, and very often, is what I call black magic. This is where we get caught up in the kind of mentality where we believe that this skill, ability, and highly trained Intuitive Intelligence help us reach our ego needs. That if we have a beautiful life, an attractive partner, a new car, lots of money in the bank, heaps of clients, then we're winning at the spiritual game. We think that that is evidence that we're doing this right. Our ego is satisfied, life is familiar, and everything is working well. We've got a massive agenda with God that goes something like this,

*You keep doing for me, and I'll do for you. If you touch a hair on the head of my babies, or you make my partner leave me, or I don't have enough clients next week, then I am out. Got it? I'm done.*

Or,

*You got to show up for me, God; I am only here whilst this works.*

We have a very shallow relationship with our awakening. We are working an agenda, whatever that agenda is. We get a little bit drunk on our power here. As a result, we think our increasing access to our intuition and co-creative capacity is evidence that we're doing good and we've got the spiritual game hacked. The point is we are falling into the trap of believing that the highest function of our spiritual awakening or our intuition is to make our human life more comfortable.

Many of us, consciously or unconsciously, use spiritual tools to manifest what we believe we should be getting. We turn up to our spirituality — and yoga and green juices and meditation and mindfulness — with the idea that we're going to be rewarded. This is maybe not something we're comfortable with hearing. Still, it is accurate, and it is a shadow side or a black magic use of the spiritual tools to try to coerce or manipulate the cosmos, the Superconscious Mind, into meeting our egoic needs.

It is a stage in our development. Let's not stop here as so many do. Let's move to align with our soul's needs. The *spiritualised ego* (to use Adyashanti's term) believes it needs this much money, this kind of book contract, this many people following us, this many people on our Instagram account to be recognised as spiritually successful. But the soul doesn't need the local reality to recognise it at all. Tibetan Buddhist spiritual leader Chögyam Trungpa wrote,

*Walking the spiritual path properly is a very subtle process: it is not something to jump into naively. There are numerous sidetracks which lead to a distorted, ego-centered version of spirituality; we can deceive ourselves into thinking*

*we are developing spirituality when instead we are strengthening our egocentricity through spiritual techniques[20].*

Our attempts to meet our local needs are only ever an attempt to meet our soul needs, even if we do not know it. When our soul needs are met, all of our ideas of a well-lived life and a successful life fall away. This is the purpose of us committing to awakening our intuition. It is not so that we can guess people's futures, and I use that word 'guess' quite intentionally. Or to be able to predict what's going to happen with COVID-19, or to be able to attract the most clients, but rather that we get closer to the truth that all is one and I am one with the mind of God.

In the light form, this is the phase of intuition in which we're starting to own that we are that. We are one with the Superconscious Mind, and we can create, not simply react.

When we start to mature and take on more of spiritual agency, in other words, become more soul identified, through our practices of showing up intentionally, actively, and in a participatory way, we begin to surrender more into the understanding that,

*Maybe this is not about getting my ego's needs met. Maybe I actually need to get out of the way a little bit more. And maybe if something "goes wrong", that's only as I'm judging it from my limited human perspective. But actually, maybe, this is just the action that needed to occur to help evolve my consciousness.*

Remembering intuition is not the thing we're seeking more of. We think we are, but we are all pursuing the same thing. And that is the raising of our consciousness back to the truth of

---

20 Chögyam Trungpa, *Cutting Through Spiritual Materialism*, 2002.

what we are, which is God. Intuition is just a great measure of that journey.

As these phases of intuition move into more sophisticated states of being, the percentage of the population that operates from them significantly decreases. Fewer people are aware of these higher levels of intuition. Most conversations and research about intuition in the world is about the biological forms of intuition. At communion intuition, we're introducing the nonlocal; we're introducing the fact that we have understanding or insight or inspiration that isn't coming through cause and effect; it's coming because we connect to that quantum field. We can know things without going to the location, without doing research, and without conversation. The information lands through our dominant intuitive skill, whole and complete within us.

We must be very, very careful here not to stop. If we look at this as a measure of spiritual agency or spiritual maturity, this is the phase of

*I'm in partnership with God.*

But the best is yet to come.

## Surrender intuition

**Qualities: subconscious, active, nonlocal, acausal, creative, full spiritual agency, deep**

Surrender intuition is when our superconscious intuition becomes our dominant subconscious program. We are running the program of intuition dominantly in our subconscious. It is entirely nonlocal. We are in symbolic sight; we're not looking at the local to give us data about the world.

We are in a state of being in which our arms are wide open, holding nothing back, saying,

*Okay, God, I'm yours. Use me.*

Our life is in service to the greater good. We have put down all agendas on how we think life should look. We've put down the idea that there's a reward system for being a good spiritual person. We stop the falsehood of believing that doing our devotion and showing up to our spiritual practices or being nice to people will be rewarded. We no longer imagine a karmic reward system and that we are supposed to get good things if we show up to God.

When we recognise that even though we do not always understand the events of our life and the events of the world around us, we trust, we surrender. We throw our arms wide open to the will of the Superconscious Mind. We are here as holy servants, Gods' humble hands and feet in the world. We don't take the events of our lives personally.

Our intuition has the most precise possible channel because we don't argue with what we receive. The endpoint of intuition is that there is no need for intuition. Surrender intuition is a step on that path. Surrender intuition is the absolute lack of resistance. It is defenselessness. Nothing could happen in our lives that we consider has gone wrong. It's a state of being. It is living in Intuitive Intelligence.

Unlike the other phases, living this state of being is something we aren't dropping in and out of when we want to know the answer to a question or feel confused and conflicted with events in our lives. We are aware simply through living in this state of being that we're in flow with the Superconscious Mind. We know when we're out of this phase of intuition by the stirrings and agitations to our state of being and recognise we

108

need to come back into flow. We do this by meeting our subconscious fear.

In this phase of intuition, we are in servitude to God, which is to say to the awakening consciousness of all. The more we awaken to our spiritual maturity, the more responsibility we want to take to ensure the dream that we're all part of is evolving on behalf of all. We are no longer seeking our gain. Our holy task is to develop our intuition so that we live in a state of being, in surrender intuition all of the time. It's a fearless state because we trust our superconscious intuition all of the time. We don't question it, even if what we're asked to do by our intuition will take us away from the familiar and the known of our comfort/familiar zone.

We might resist being in surrender intuition because we are so suspicious of being tuned in all the time to our intuition. We think that means it's about getting information about other people and the world all of the time, and that we will be exhausted by that responsibility. It isn't. That is absolutely the opposite of the truth, and it is born of our separation mentality and the false idea that we need to protect ourselves from others. We're interested in understanding that there is only one of us here and that we aren't trying to defend ourselves energetically from everyone else. Instead we hold a vibration that is so high and light that we bring everyone else into it and entrain them to the superconscious frequency. It is effortless. It is flow.

Surrender intuition in its light form is complete trust in the Superconscious Mind and living in the flow state. It is 100% soul-identified. Living this state of being can only exist through consistent devotion. It doesn't happen randomly. It's a refined state of being that requires congruence. Most of us are not there yet. Our aim and the measure of our spiritual agency is to live in surrender intuition as often as possible. Even if it means that my ego will be throwing tantrums left, right and centre, I'm not going to put down my faith just because it's awkward, uncomfortable or inconvenient.

In its shadow form, surrender intuition can see us wanting to withdraw from the world, bypassing our humanity. We say,

*I want to be in meditation, in a cave on top of a mountain where it feels so good to be in the presence of God, away from all of you human folk who are just bringing me down with your human dramas.*

We attempt to withdraw instead of taking God out into the world. We say things that bypass other people's experiences. We will negate people or ourselves and not allow our humanity to be present in our divinity. This is problematic because we're in a human experience for an excellent reason. The shadow form of surrender intuition is where we abdicate responsibility for showing up to the state of the world.

We may also find that this is a point where we have a spiritual crisis because we feel like,

*I don't want to be here anymore. Just take me back, God. I just want to be with you now.*

Many of us have experienced that in different ways, that grief of separation from God. It's something I've experienced. I remember even as a little child looking up at the sky and feeling,

*Why am I down here and you're up there?*

Even then, I felt that there was separation from my truth, expansiveness, and bigness. But I didn't know how to name it, even though the truth is I am never not with God.

Yet another shadow of surrender intuition is that we become unintentionally passive and reject responsibility. I have seen this happen where we assume that everything will be taken care of by God, and we don't need to take action or show up to our lives proactively. We might become apathetic and wait on the will of heaven.

For example, a woman recently was about to join one of the Institute's programs. I knew it was a profound, intuitively guided decision for her, but it was going to take her whole life commitment and turn things upside down. She went to pay the initial deposit for the program, and she entered incorrect credit card details. When my team contacted her to let her know, she said,

*Oh, it's a sign. God doesn't want me to do this.*

I thought,

*Maybe, or maybe this is just you now sitting in such a passive state that you are assuming everything is God's will as a way to avoid taking action. Committing to this program presented an opportunity to meet your fear. Maybe it wasn't right for you to go ahead, but there's a good chance that maybe it was, and this was just an unmet subconscious fear about moving closer to divine truth.*

I adore the saying — trust in God but tie up your camel — an ancient Arabic phrase attributed to Mohammed. One day Mohammed saw a Bedouin leaving his camel without tethering it and questioned him why he was doing this. The Bedouin replied that he trusted Allah and had no need to tie the camel. The prophet Mohammed replied, 'Tie your camel and place your trust in Allah'.[21] We should have faith that everything will

---

21 Accessed at: https://www.carleton.edu/chaplain/news/trust-in-god-and-tie-your-camel/

work out, but at the same time do what we can to ensure a favourable outcome. If we let the shadow of surrender intuition make us passive, we have missed the point. Surrender is not passive. Active faith requires us to take God-inspired action in the world.

A student of mine was recently in a housing crisis. Along with her large family and many pets, she moved at short notice. I was well aware of this crisis and was impressed to see her thinking divergently and creating out of the box intuitively guided choices that would ensure her life was a better match for her desired lifestyle. Changes were put in place, and choices were made. But as the date to move grew close, with only a week to go, she suddenly became very passive. The place she was meant to move to was not yet ready, and she wasn't getting the support she needed from her partner to get the place ready. She shared this with me and when I asked her why she didn't just take charge, she replied that she had faith that God would provide. My response was exactly the Arabic phrase from above. I emphatically asked her to help God out and to play her part. Within hours, that was exactly what she did.

This is such a clear example of surrender intuition in its shadow. If we are standing in the middle of traffic, trusting that God will ensure the cars and trucks don't hit us, we'd be wiser to be God for ourselves and get the hell off the road.

When we move into surrender intuition, we're living from that expansive state. In fact, surrender intuition is anchoring into all of our intuitions, and living from all of them in their light form. This allows us to indeed come into our highest state of being of intuitive intelligence.

## How to work with the four phases

I want us to understand this map because it's not a ladder, just as the chakras are not a ladder. We evolve through our chakras, just as we evolve through these phases of intuition. At any given time, we might be in a different phase of intuition in any different life situation.

For example, in our career and professional life, we might be connected to our superconscious intuition — we're in communion intuition, we're able to connect into our meditative state easily and divine the correct next best steps for our life. But when it comes to our personal relationships, we're a bloody nightmare. We don't decide without seeing a psychic tell us if we should be going out with that person or not. Because we're so caught up in all of the emotional chaos of our love life that we've got no clarity. We're in reactive intuition when it comes to that. Likewise, when we care about things very deeply, for example, our children, we might be very, very afraid that they're not safe. We're in our primary intuition, in dysregulation, constantly in that state of fear that something bad will happen to them because our love is fear.

With this map, we're not saying,

*Oh, my God, I have to get to the final phase of intuition; otherwise, I've failed as a spiritual being.*

Instead, this is a way for us to measure our evolution.

*What level of spiritual agency am I bringing to this event in this particular life situation? Am I in my victim? Am I sitting in a reactive state? Or am I actually able to see that there may be a higher purpose to what is happening and that if I can find my way into my devotion, I may be able to hear that God voice that is guiding me with the next best steps.*

113

Another reason we will often resist evolving our intuition is that we don't like what our intuition is telling us. And we'll say,

*Oh, I can't tell what my intuition says. Oh no, I can't hear it.*

What we're doing is this. We're putting our hands over our ears and shaking our heads and mumbling,

*Can't hear it, can't hear it.*

We don't want to hear it. Because it's obvious what's next, and what's next might be that we have to get out of our comfort/familiar zone. We have to leave behind our littleness and go towards our gloriousness because, remember, intuition is a byproduct of awakening to our soul nature, and our soul is glorious. Anywhere we are sitting in our littleness or our comfort or our reactive state, we will be agitated out of that by our intuition. Intuition is never going to be comfortable and rarely going to give us,

*Oh, you're doing great. Just keep doing that same old thing you've always been doing.*

No, it's not going to do that. Once we open honestly to our intuition, we are constantly invited to move beyond our limits. That is what intuition is about; it is how to evolve our soul, not comfort our ego. And as we've said before, comfort is a misnomer anyway. When we seek comfort in a dream, we are literally out of our minds. Because we don't tell our little children when they are in a nightmare,

*Oh my God, yes, the monsters are really going to get you! Quickly run.*

We say,

*Hey, baby, it's okay. You're just dreaming. Everything's fine. Wake up, mama's here. You're in my arms. You're completely safe.*

That is the truth of what we are doing in this human consciousness experiment — we are dreaming ourselves awake. And when we're seeking for the dream to keep us asleep because it's so comfortable, we're in a paradox that cannot be sustained. We must get good with being uncomfortable. Intuition is only going to increase our discomfort, but blessedly it's also going to raise our awareness of our divine and holy nature. And that ultimately is the only comfort we need.

## Deep versus shallow intuition

Those of us who are called to serve through our intuition have a responsibility to keep seeking to go deeper with our intuition. We must not stay in the shallow end. A shallow versus a deep state of intuition is really about the level of consciousness that we're accessing. A deep state of intuition is not something we go into and come out of, but a shallow state of intuition is. The statements that typify a shallow state include,

*I just have to check in with my intuition. I just need to ask a question. I'm just going to tune in and get a download.*

These statements indicate that a person is in a shallow state of intuition. What we aim for when we do the deep work of deep faith is to live in connection to our superconscious intuition, the state of being we call Intuitive Intelligence, to Oneness all of the time. We don't step in, ask a question, and go back to being tuned out. We reside in it all of the time. There's no question to even ask. We want to be 'tuned' in constantly, always in a flow state of Intuitive Intelligence,

115

which is the absolute certainty with every breath that this is the right place. This is the right moment, and if that starts to feel wrong, then we course correct, but we don't stop, pause, ask, leave. We want to be in a flow state. We want to be constantly floating in that beautiful deep state.

We stay in the shallow end of our intuition and choose to 'tune' in, ask the pendulum or pull the card because it gives us a false sense of authority and control. At the same time, it is abdicating us of any responsibility. What do I mean by that? We get this sense that we can actively command intuition to show up when we want it, which is the false sense of control because whilst intuition is always instant, it isn't on demand. It's instant when it decides to land.

The other aspect of that is it's us saying,

*Well, something outside of me knows more.*

Even if we're referencing our intuition as the thing outside of us that we connect to, we're still going outside of us. We never want to be out of tune with our highest form of Intelligence.

A shallow state of intuition includes when we are still identifying intuition as a third eye chakra function. Yet the third eye is the periscope and not the source of our intuition. As we learned in Chapter Two, a deep state of intuition is anchored in the heart (chakra and brain). The third eye is the symbolic interpreter of our heart's nonlocal intuition. It's where the deep state of intuition generated by the heart emerges in our subtle body so that we can receive the symbolic sight, but it's not the origin of it. Let me break that down a little bit here.

To stop, think about an issue, ask a question in regards to that issue, and do whatever processes we do to get into our intuitive state; light a candle, burn some incense, meditate, draw a card, whatever, we have to have been out of our intuition. We've gone straight into our Reasoning Conscious Mind to engage in these practices. When we tune in and out of our intuition, this automatically moves us into the analytical brain's Conscious Reasoning Mind. We've shut down our natural innate ability to connect to the deep states of intuition. We're in our analytical brain. We've engaged the ego-identity self to access something below the Conscious Reasoning Mind. We've already created a schism or a dissonance in how we're accessing our intuition. We have engaged in analytical processing. When we've leapt into our Conscious Reasoning Mind to receive our intuition, we have returned to the state of being that we may live in most of the time, so it is a continuation of what feels familiar and comfortable. We prefer the control or perceived authority of this shallow state of intuition to turn on or off our intuition.

## Intuition is not in the dream

As we've discussed in communion intuition, we'll see signs everywhere when we realise we create all of them ourselves. There is no symbol that we're going to see that will confirm our intuition; there's no sign that will prove our intuition one way or another because deep states of intuition are internal. They are an aspect of our soul; they have nothing to do with the dream.

The dream is not a function of deep states of intuition. When we see confirmation in the dream, we are undoubtedly in a shallow state of intuition. We've privileged the illusion as a way to evidence what we now are taking as confirmation of our 'intuition'. If we're looking externally in any way, including for 'signs' to confirm the world, we are in a shallow state of intuition.

What are we doing in a deep state of intuition, then? That is when we are in our highest form of intelligence, our heart's intelligence, which is below the Conscious Reasoning Mind. This is a function of our subconscious. Our subconscious is where we want to be operating from. The ego cannot hijack us then. Intuition cannot be interpreted by the analytical, critical part of our brain trying to make reason out of something that functions outside of reason. It is nonlocal.

Intuitive Intelligence doesn't have a relationship with the local world. Deep states of intuition come from the nonlocal field, with no need for the dream of this life to produce any evidence at all. We draw upon the Superconscious Mind when we are in that right relationship with the subconscious. We're not drawing upon our prior history, our association with what that butterfly means, or what that number on the clock indicates. Instead, we are one with the deep state of nonlocal communication, connected with that Superconscious Mind, connected to all time and all space.

We're drawing on wisdom, which is, yes, paradoxically us, but below the level of our identity, our personality. We're sitting in a much deeper state, accessed by showing up to devotion and creating a regulated nervous system. Very often, I hear people associating their shallow states of intuition with signs that are a dysregulated nervous system, and I'm like,

*Oh, nope, that wasn't your intuition. That was your unregulated nervous system.*

A regulated nervous system allows us to live from our intuition, from the subconscious, without our ego identity getting in the way by trying to make associations and interpretations of signs through its foggy lens. Recently, a student in my year-long traineeship dropped out at the halfway point. She had been struggling with dysregulation initially, and we were working to support her with this. We were making great inroads to bring her out of 'hiding' from this dysregulation, which meant she kept wanting to disappear from the group so she didn't have to commit to the process. Some days she was all in and experiencing a sense of breakthrough, and other days, she vanished. So I shouldn't have been too surprised when she contacted me to advise that she had to follow her 'truth' to leave the program.

My alarm bells went off. The shadow this student had been working with from the beginning of the program was the good girl archetype and associated behaviour of people-pleasing. She found her inner spiritual authority, and it was beautiful to see. The program firmly held her to do so.

Her sudden decision to leave was the ego attempting to control this process. To the ego in shadow, I became the symbol of all the people she had ever tried to please. The ego wanted her out because if she kept going on the path of awakening, she would be genuinely free of the 'good girl' program. The ego convinced her that I was the problem, the program was, or the mentors, whatever it may be, so she stopped the awakening process. The ego was masquerading as intuition, and my student was utterly convinced.

Why did this happen? Why couldn't she see the power play at work in her consciousness? As I mentioned earlier, this student was dysregulated at times, and despite the enormous effort she put in, she needed more time to heal this response. The ego didn't want that. Control was slipping from its clutches, and so often, what happens for all of us when we feel this is that we just want to do something, *anything*, to feel back in control once more. She had committed to the program from her Intuitive Intelligence, and I watched throughout as her ego attempted to wrestle her back into the comfort/familiar zone. My student was retreating to the familiar and the known under the ego's machinations masquerading as intuition.

So what's the antidote? We want to make our intuition a subconscious process. We want to live in it all of the time. Why would we stop, pause, tune in and then tune out when our intuition is a subconscious program running in the background all of the time? We wouldn't. It's the dominant program. We make it the dominant program by meeting our fear every damn day. The subconscious MUST be regulated. The nervous system is the expression of the subtle body's health. Regulating the nervous system, by meeting and releasing trauma and fear, is how we come into these deep states of intuition. A dysregulated nervous system is an expression of a cluttered subconscious; this cluttered subconscious is the expression of our subtle body. We cannot receive these deep states of intuition without coming into a regulated nervous system.

When we move out of our deep states of intuition, we get a fear jolt. Or we might suddenly go into doubt, or we'll go into worry. There's some good intel that we've stepped out of our deep state of intuition. We've stepped out of our dominant subconscious program. We recognise we need to course-correct, do the damn work and come back into it. We aren't answering a question about who we should marry, if we should join this, or if we should not do that. We are living in a flow state, all of the time unfettered by the dream of this life. We are not seeking specific answers for specific questions because we simply don't need to. We know that the second we feel we have moved out of flow, good intel is coming to us. Remember our fear is intuitive intel, highlighting that something needs to be course-corrected. We are in tune all of the time, and when we feel out of tune, we restore the right action and come back into that deep state. See the difference?

To live in a deep state of intuition, to have our nervous system regulated, the subconscious primed, released from fear, running the dominant intuition program, tuned in all of the time, is what we call Intuitive Intelligence. This is when our Intuitive Intelligence has become our state of being.

That's what we are aiming for with our life. That's why we are doing the damn work every damn day to get clear of those faulty programs that keep us out of the state of being we want to live in. We know that our physiology is the technology to access those deep states of intuition. We need to be unafraid to engage that, but not from a local perspective. Let's dive deeper into the relationship between the nervous system and intuition.

# Chapter 6

# Our Biology is the Technology of our Intuition

*"Through his famous equation E=mc², Albert Einstein proved to scientists that energy and matter are dual expressions of the same universal substance. That universal substance is a primal energy or vibration of which we are all composed".*

—*Richard Gerber*

I want to introduce the relationship between our body, nervous system, and Intuitive Intelligence. Intuitive Intelligence is an embodied state of being. Our biology, our body, and in particular, our nervous system, is the technology of our Intuitive Intelligence.

We can think about the nervous system as the interface between the physical and subtle bodies. It carries electrical information through our biology. When we have a dysregulated nervous system, telling someone to trust their intuition, especially in a crisis, is like telling someone to pick up a jumbo jet. It's simply impossible. Even if we can receive our intuition through all the chaos of a dysregulated nervous system, we will be in such a state of uncertainty within ourselves that we will not necessarily have the faith or courage to act on it.

We've all had experiences where we know we've received intuitive understanding. Still, we've doubted ourselves. We've gone into our rational brain or let other people's opinions influence us. We've made lists of good or bad. We've discounted that intuitive knowing because there's no space inside of us to feel certainty. When intuition lands into a regulated nervous system, we will have a sense of anchoring or groundedness. We will often mistake impulsive heightened emotional decisions for intuition when in dysregulation. There are many aspects to how a dysregulated nervous system can mislead us. We think that our intuition is guiding, and it's our dysregulation. Deep subconscious programs that are unmet are often doing the talking and masquerading as intuition. I'm going to get to the antidote for all of this, by the way, so don't fear. If we're sitting here going,

*How am I ever supposed to trust my intuition?*

Let me offer a personal example.

Many years ago, when I was in the early stages of my relationship with my husband, I felt very strongly that this kind, loving, intelligent, stable man was all wrong for me. I knew 'intuitively' that I needed to break up with him, which I did. I found all sorts of reasons he was no good for me, even though I was really happy and deeply in love. We were looking to create a fantastic future together. But I ended it guided by 'intuitive knowing'.

Many months later, I had not recovered from my feelings for him. I'd broken up with him, but I hadn't moved on. I was just dismal. I asked myself,

*Why am I so despairing and heartbroken if my intuition guided me to leave this man?*

It took some deep self-reflection and self-investigation to understand that I had, at that time, a powerful fear of being disapproved of. This fear of disapproval was so strong in me, albeit subconsciously, that having someone so approving of me felt foreign. To my ego, it was dangerous because it felt like a trick. I am not approvable. Yet, here's this person approving me just as I am.

I was able to explore and excavate the subconscious fear. The discomfort of breaking my own heart provided the grounds for my liberation. I came back to the truth through devotion and commitment to uncovering this program and going through processes that helped me change that pattern. Through spiritual sweat, I recognised that I am approved of, and not just by him, but *by myself.* I was very blessed that he could let me back into his heart, even though I triggered his fear of betrayal. However, we went on and were able to heal those wounds together and grow the strength of our relationship.

It's our holy task to sit with the discomfort of,

*My intuition might be dysregulated.*

We need to be willing to do the deep work of deep faith. We need to overcome our superficial relationship with our intuition, which has been all about getting our ego's needs met. We need to mature our relationship with our intuition and recognise that sometimes our intuitive knowledge will make us more uncomfortable than comfortable as we evolve.

Where does that leave us? How do we ever learn to trust ourselves?

Intuition is our highest form of intelligence. Our nervous system is the receiver of intuition into our physiology. When it's all working, it is the shortcut to the best life we've ever lived. But when we have an untrained relationship with our intuition, which is to say we don't know how to bring ourselves into regulation, we will either misrepresent our intuition or be bamboozled about why our intuition would guide us to make certain choices.

We know by now that our Intuitive Intelligence is about our evolution, not our comfort. Yet, we often 'check in' with our intuition because we want to get the guarantee that everything's going to work out. We'll go to a psychic or an intuitive reader or a healer, or our tarot cards because we want a sense of control by trying to know the answers in advance.

We will often be agitated by what our intuition guides us to know. This is yet another way we reject our intuition, even when it's right, because it might be asking us to see the truth. Intuition shows us that the relationship is not good for us or that the job is killing us. But our fear gets loud.

*How will I survive? How would I live without that person? How could I possibly go forward in my life without all of these things that I think keep me safe?*

We know what our intuition is saying. But because of those fears of the future or projections into the past, we're unable to trust what we're receiving. Our dysregulation is often caused because we are not in present time. And if we are not in present time we are not home to receive our intuition.

## The timeliness of Intuitive Intelligence

Intuition is only available to us in the present time. Intuitive intelligence is a function of quantum reality. In a quantum understanding of the universe, all is one. All time and space is one. There is no past, and there is no future. When we tap into that Superconscious Mind, that field of information that contains all we need, all the great spiritual teachers advocate for presence. But as an aspect of intuition, it's vital. If we are obsessed with past events, living our history, not letting go of things, unforgiving, holding on to our pain, then we are not home. We are not present. Likewise, if we're constantly terrified of the future, we're never available in the present. When we're in fear of what has happened to us in the past or what might happen to us in the future, we aren't present.

We must be willing to cultivate presence as part of our commitment to increasing our access to our Intuitive Intelligence. In creating an ecology for the natural development of our Intuitive Intelligence, slowing down is a critical piece of the puzzle. A life full of rushing and structured activity does not permit us to expand into full presence in this moment now. When we rush ourselves from pillar to post, feeling stress and urgency in every moment, we are not present. Presence means allowing each moment to guide us to the best course of action. When we allow ourselves to be present, we tune in to what we feel bodily, emotionally, and energetically. Without that, we can overtax the nervous system and live in our sympathetic nervous system response – fight, flight or freeze – even when we are not in a life-threatening situation. Stress reduces our capacity to connect to our Intuitive Intelligence. The high beta brainwave state that we are in when we are in our sympathetic nervous system closes off the communication between the heart and cranial brains.

# A conversation with embodiment expert Elisha Halpin

No discussion of the intersections of intuition and nervous system regulation would be complete without the wisdom of my friend and colleague, Elisha Halpin. Elisha is bringing a new perspective to this leading-edge field. Elisha is breaking new ground with her work, and it is a great privilege to bring her work to a new audience through this interview.

I first connected with Elisha through my online community, I am Spiritually Fierce. I was instantly impressed with the quality of her contribution to the conversation on intuition. As a fellow academic, I was excited by the rigour she brought to the ideas she shared. I invited her to be a guest speaker at the Intuitive Intelligence Symposium in Tuscany in 2018. As with many other speakers, I assumed she would present virtually rather than make the long journey from her home in State College, Pennsylvania.

Instead, Elisha jumped at the opportunity to embrace her passion, travelling, especially on spiritual pilgrimages. It turned out to be a divinely fated meeting. Elisha and I first lay eyes on each other in real life outside of a *chiosco* in a tiny Tuscan village late at night as she climbed out of a taxi that had transported her from the local train station. We embraced with such warmth and familiarity it was as though we were meeting after a few days apart, not for the first time.

We both sensed that we had big work to do together, and it is in combining our shared passion for spiritually mature teaching of intuition development. Elisha's expertise in embodiment and nervous system regulation, and deep commitment to her spiritual awakening, marries with the theory and praxis of Intuitive Intelligence. The basis of Elisha's work is Intuitive Intelligence, energy science, Neurosculpting, and somatic embodiment, using tools such as daily rituals, embodied practice, breathwork, journaling, connecting to divine feminine power, neuro-repatterning, and energy healing. She is a dance professor and a high priestess. Elisha is of mixed race of Cherokee, Scotch-Irish, and African descent. She leads from a Celtic Spiritual path but invites the interweaving of the sacred practices of all her ancestors. It is precisely because of all these intersections of her identity and service that Elisha brings such a rich and dynamic perspective to this conversation.

Because of Elisha's teachings, I understood that Intuitive Intelligence is an *embodied state of being*. So, I couldn't share further information on this subject without inviting Elisha directly into the book.

### R: What's exciting or agitating you about nervous system regulation and intuition development right now?

E: There's a lot of mainstream hype about regulation. Most people are learning about their nervous system right now on Instagram. The way it's presented is that you're either regulated or dysregulated. We know that some of us might have a certain regulation, and some might have a certain dysregulation. Part of getting in touch with your regulation is understanding the multifaceted parts of you, right? We're not looking to get it right.

One of the biggest things that keep people from living into a fuller or higher regulation is they want to be right. They're protecting *being right*, which means that they want to put on a facade of what regulation is, rather than looking at it as energetic frequency creating coherence or creating dissonance in our system.

Regulation is not about removing the dissonance or pretending that there isn't dissonance. It's working with the dissonance to bring it into coherence. If we're not afraid of dissonance in our system, then we're not pretending that we wouldn't be dissonant.

**R: It's the same conversation, as fear is a friendly ally. Dysregulation is the tap on the shoulder saying, hey, Ricci-Jane...**

E: Do you want to get more regulated? Do you recognise you're out of alignment? Did you notice that you shut down? Fear is the way that the story shows up. How do I meet the dysregulation? How do I support myself into a higher level of frequency?

What I'm really curious about right now in this journey of regulation is how do we learn to meet the dysregulation in a way that we're opening up sustainably and incrementally? Rather than doing what most people have been taught to do, which is live in their dissonance, their disconnect, their fear, their dysregulation, and then pop briefly into regulation. They shoot up to a high frequency, but they can't sustain it. All they're doing is shooting to the top of their system and then plummeting back to the bottom and going on a crazy journey. It keeps the reactive intuition as the norm. It keeps us addicted to energetic sensitivity as a way of being rather than knowing energetic sensitivity is no different from me smelling using my nose. My energetic senses are as normal as my physical senses, and also they need to be integrated. Otherwise, how do we know what's true?

The other aspect around regulation that I'm curious about right now is this understanding that you might be regulating to fear. You can regulate to fear, or you can regulate to Bliss. Part of the co-regulation aspect is that it is always happening. And if we're not conscious about it, we're all going to be falling into our inertia. We're going to be falling into entropy. We will regulate down into the mediocre middle.

One of the things that I think is so important to remember is that entropy is stronger than evolution. The impulse to entropy is always stronger. Evolution is the counter. It's the swimming upstream. So it takes more energy. It takes more awareness. It takes more consciousness. And that's why so many of us continue to fall into our own pits. We haven't cultivated enough inner strength in our nervous system to swim upstream. The current of human consciousness right now is headed downward. When we recognise that *my job, my self-responsibility in my own regulation journey, is to cultivate an ability to hold my inner alignment, I am in service. It doesn't mean I'm going to be perfect. It doesn't mean I'm not going to yell at my kids*. It doesn't mean all of these things that we want to make regulation about. It's about holding my inner alignment. It's about having the strength to stay congruent.

We have this idea that the shadow, dysregulation, or the mundane is different from the light. What happens is we're negating at least half of life. That means that my nervous system is now no longer open to the experience that life is bringing me. When something challenging happens, when I have a loss, when I hit grief, when I hit difficulty, when the waters get choppy, I'm not prepared to stay open. I'm not available to life. The majority of people are only available for what's good. I'm living in addition to my *like*. I like this experience. I like being happy, right? The path of non-duality is about the integration of all of life. My grief is no different than my ecstasy. They are simply experiences that I'm having. I don't have an opinion about those experiences.

I'm able to be inside of them. I experienced grief. It hurts. It was sad. I was *that,* right? I was ecstatic. It was blissful. It was joyful. I was that. I am all of it. If we're only seeking peak experiences, what we're saying is the rest of life doesn't matter. This is one reason why privilege and separation between those that have and those that don't continue. We have not harmonised within ourselves, *the orphan, the thief, the perpetrator,* these parts of our system that we don't want to come into integration with.

Embodiment is where I make space to be with the part of me that was orphaned. I make space for the part of me that was the bully, is the bully, is bullying myself, all of those things. Embodiment is about making space for every single archetype. This particular life journey might be about several of those archetypes expressed explicitly. But ultimately, I am all of that. If I can accept my bully, I don't have to orient towards that bully. I just get that a part of me can bully myself or could bully somebody else. This means that when I see that mirror in the world, rather than seeing it as separate, I check in with myself. *Oh, where am I? Where am I still carrying resonance to that if I see it in the world? There's a resonance in me. It's still in me, right? I'm still in resonance with that.*

To believe that we have to have a peak experience to get closer to God creates a false notion of what God is.

**R: Speak to me about your perspective, your spiritual perspective, on what the nervous system is.**

The nervous system is the channel tuner or the antenna. It sits listening inside this body and helping to tune my biochemistry and my physical anatomy. It's listening to my subtle body and drawing the information in, and tuning me to my subtle body. And it's listening in to the nonlocal expanded self, and it's tuning into the universal field.

The nervous system is the two-way highway of receiving and giving energy and information. It's constantly sending messages to all the parts and layers of my system. It's not just in this physical form. The nervous system's job is to move the energy it receives in all the directions that it needs to, and it is always listening and interpreting. Some people say the body doesn't lie.

I disagree. The body lies. Because when your nervous system is tuned to fear, that's a lie because the only truth is love. So if I've gone through trauma, if I've come through conditioning that makes me fearful of the world, if I'm living in stuckness, smallness and stagnation, my body's going to lie to me. My body lies to me about the illnesses I'm holding. My body lies to me about the way it's reading energetics because it is tuned to fear. It is tuned to mistrust and gloom and all the fear. If I want to trust my body, I want to orient my nervous system's tuning into love and expansion into higher consciousness. The nervous system is the interface of consciousness.

As it moves into the brain, our nervous system gives us a field of perception, how we see and experience. When information about fear is coming into the brain, the way the story gets told is through this perception of fear. This means that I'm then sending out that electromagnetic signature, which means I'm getting met by that electromagnetic signature. This means that I take in that information, and it confirms my belief! I get weighed down.

I speak about the *nervous system load*. How loaded is the nervous system? If there's a lot of static in our nervous systems, it's almost like your eyelids are only partially open. The more you unload the nervous system, the more the eyes can open. With many people, when they go through an awakening to their intuition, their eyes are half-open. They call that good enough, and I find those people the most dangerous. Half-awake. When you're half-open, and you think you know something, and you think you're moving from your truth, but you're only seeing through part of your vision because your nervous system is still loaded, you're very dangerous. You're drawing in that information into your nervous system. But it's got to go through all of your static. What happens a lot is that people have some awakening, and then they want to be done. They want to be good enough. But they don't do the full work of unloading the nervous system so that they can receive the truth through eyes wide open. If we're not unloading the static, then what happens is you can't trust what's coming back out of your mouth. It goes through distortion because your system is not clear. Unloading the nervous system is the only way to become a clear channel.

If you're choosing the path of transformation, you are under a sacred obligation to heal your nervous system. And by healing, you are removing those blocks where the energy is not flowing. Our sacred obligation is to undo those knots because it is the only way to become a superregulator, which means my nervous systems are unloaded and accessible and I am able to support others to find a greater regulation. Service is having our energy system, our house, in order. Only when my house is in order can I say *I can open this house to others*. Too often, we don't want to get deep enough or raw enough inside our own nervous system work. We want to make it about everybody else. And that is where we're not in service of the collective. If my house is not in order, I cannot hold that many people in my house. My job is to hold the whole world, which means my nervous system has to be open and available. I can't be hiding behind being an empath. I have to take these things that I've decided were kryptonite and make them into a superpower. I have to be willing to get more serious about the work. That is the gauntlet that we have to throw, especially to spiritually privileged white women. You're not doing the work deep enough. You're playing on the surface, and you want to express before you've embodied. You want it to look great on Instagram. That's why the world does not trust you right now and that's why you're not making an impact.

## Acknowledge. Regulate. Connect

Any practices that keep us out of the fight, flight or freeze response will increase our access to our intuition. Methods of meditation, chanting, yoga, exercising, anything that helps keep us in homeostasis supports our Intuitive Intelligence technology. Conversely, suppose we are in an abusive relationship with our bodies. In that case, it's doubtful that we're going to receive our intuition in a way that we can feel confident. This body is the receiver, and we must honour that. A few minutes each day of silence, stillness and solitude, slowing down the brainwave state, slowing down the heart rate, and allowing the body to come into a feeling of safety are all necessary precursors to a deep state of intuition.

Generally, to withdraw our attention from the external world for at least a few minutes every day and to shut down those external senses to go within is vital to establishing a deep intuition. To regulate the breath, and to use the breath in a way that stimulates the vagus nerve, in particular, is vital. Stimulation through diaphragmatic breathing — by filling the belly as much as possible — helps keep us in our parasympathetic nervous system.

When we are committed to regulating our nervous system, our Intuitive Intelligence increases. The process of ARC — Acknowledge, regulate and connect — is designed to bring us into a regulated state to have the most accurate connection to our Intuitive Intelligence.

**Step One**. The first letter A stands for **acknowledge**. To receive our intuition and trust it, we have to acknowledge what state we're in at the point of seeking access to our intuition.

*Am I in a panic? Am I afraid? Am I stressed out? Am I feeling out of control?* If I acknowledge where I'm at in my state of being, I can change my state of being through the second step, **regulation**.

**Step Two.** This step involves engaging in any practice that supports regulation in the body. I recommend diaphragmatic breathing, closing the eyes, silence, tapping, meditation, chanting, toning, amongst many other possibilities.

Most likely, for many of us, no matter where we are in our day, there's always a benefit to engaging in practices that will bring us a little more deeply into regulation.

**Step Three**. We **connect**. The truth is we are always connected to our intuition, but now we are focussed with conscious intention and attention on cultivating the state of being of Intuitive Intelligence.

Here I recommend placing your hand at the centre of your chest. When we place our hand here, we acknowledge our heart-brain as the centre of our Intuitive Intelligence and anchor into what Megan Watterson calls the Cathedral of the heart. We breathe into this centre. If there is a particular life situation that we're seeking guidance around, we simply hold that in our mind as we hold our attention on our heart in our regulated biology. We feel that sense of expansion that comes when we slow everything down. Letting that Intuitive Intelligence come to you in whatever way it will, feeling, hearing, seeing or knowing. The feeling will always bring a sense of certainty, anchoring, and deepening.

I invite us all to use this process for ourselves before we inquire into our intuition. *Acknowledge, regulate, and then connect.* Do this every day. I thoroughly recommend it because regulating our nervous systems and connecting to our intuition will always yield tremendous benefits even if there isn't a particular question or any particular challenge in our life.

# Chapter 7

# What is a Trinket and Superstition of the new age?

*"Remember this, my darling—remember this. What you achieve on earth is only a small part of the deal. If there's a secret I could whisper, and that you could keep, it would be that it's all inside you already. Every single thing you need. Earth is just a stopover. A kind of game. Make it a star game. If I could give you a gift, it would be to teach you how to stay free inside that game, to find the glory inside yourself, beyond the roles and the drama, so you can dance the dance of the game of life with a little more rhythm, a little more abandon, a little more shaking-those-hips."*

*—Annie Kagan*

A trinket or superstition is any belief, action or object to which meaning is assigned that suggests or encourages dualism. No man-made dogma or local material object contains more power than our direct connection to the nonlocal field. Let's say that another way. A trinket and superstition of the new age are` whenever we place special attention upon or privilege the local plane before the nonlocal. Whenever we believe that matter or form precedes the nonlocal or pure consciousness plane, we have it all the wrong way around. **A trinket or superstition is *everything* that separates us from oneness.** Now, let's break this down.

## Energy First, Physical Second

As quantum physics tells us, we are pure consciousness, pure energy. We are vibrating fields of energy. We look solid, but that's just because we perceive the world through our dominant five senses, which is only one kind of perception. We don't see the more significant part of us, the subtle anatomy surrounding our physical body. We only see the physical body, and we privilege that, ignoring the much larger part of ourselves. When I say I don't deal in trinkets and superstitions of the New Age, I'm saying I don't believe in physical matter as existing before my belief about it. Everything in my world behaves in accordance or in response to my thoughts about it. We are collapsing the wave function to use the language of quantum physics wherever we hold a core belief. Wherever we train our thoughts, and we have those thoughts repeatedly, we collapse all other potentials. We no longer exist in a state of infinite possibility.

Everything is but a vibration. Everything is set in motion by our feeling state. The feeling state is set in motion by beliefs. The belief is happening at the subconscious level. If we were creating reality from our Reasoning Conscious Mind alone, we'd all be living like rock stars having the best life ever with all our needs met. That's why affirmations don't work because we're trying to create from the known. As we've learnt, the subconscious is the storehouse of our beliefs, and this level of mind creates our reality. This doesn't just happen at the individual level. The creation of reality is happening at the level of the collective unconscious of all humanity. We share a collective unconscious in which we're all participating. When we change our perspective and recognise what we truly are, we change the collective unconscious. Moving beyond trinkets and superstitions is moving beyond 'you and me' as separate beings. There is only one of us here.

When we return to the quantum realm, we engineer our reality rather than just reacting to what we *also* engineered from our subconscious fear program. We have a personal responsibility to upgrade our consciousness and become a clearer vessel for superconsciousness to come through us into the world. Our task is to dissolve the boundaries between ourselves and the Superconscious Mind. If we are getting caught up in the belief that something in this material plane could in any way cause us to be less or more of anything, we've missed the point.

The local plane is here to serve our awakening consciousness. That's its job. We come to earth school to raise our consciousness to the God Mind. Everything in this local realm is here to reflect our level of consciousness and a way to awaken our consciousness. It has its own independent action *and* is a product of our beliefs. We must stay away from the belief that the solid material plane is the dominant or most valuable plane or where we go to get our healing. It isn't. If we want to heal anything in the material plane, it's an inside job. And that inside job is moving back to the truth of what we are, superconsciousness. Ultimately, to live beyond the trinkets and superstitions of the new age is to believe no longer that God is out there. We rest in the truth that *we are God.*

## Spiritual Fragility

There are many ways that we hide from the truth of oneness inside of our spirituality. One of the most common ways is that we want our spirituality and the traits we identify with spirituality to be identified as exceptional. We create a hierarchy or individuation of spiritual 'merit'. The more sensitive, fragile, or incapable of functioning in the world, the higher our spiritual merit? There is so much wrong with this idea, not least of which we have to believe that the *dream is real*. We invest in an 'us and them' mentality. These are statements laden with judgement. We are separating ourselves from the collective consciousness, falsely believing that somehow our hyper-spirituality makes us unique and different and in need of protection (we'll explore energetic protection later in the book).

We are not in oneness. We seek to be identified as more unique, sensitive, and spiritual. From believing that there is a special place in the world we need to visit to evolve our consciousness or a certain crystal that will activate our pineal gland, a sacred temple we must pray in, or a must-do retreat that will make us better meditators, to the arrangement of furniture in our house, or a rare oil, we must ingest. How often have we believed that the dream contains the answer and that the answer is *somewhere else*? How laden are these beliefs with privilege? What if I cannot, because of my gender, disability, financial status, race, sexual orientation, education level, gain access to these things? Am I less spiritual? Am I less likely to attain enlightenment in this life?

Fragility like this builds on the idea of *individual attainment* of spiritual growth. The world is a reflection of the nightmare of this individuation mentality. This is a kind of superficial spirituality, which leads us to believe that spiritual 'enlightenment' is the attainment of individual success and permits us to abdicate responsibility for the welfare of anyone or anything but our own self-centric reality. It can only ever be performative spirituality, no matter how well-intentioned that co-opts spiritual tropes to attain the appearance of wisdom, without doing the work of the spiritual seeker, and often through the cultural appropriation of indigenous people's faith and identity.

Another face of spiritual fragility is our resistance to be humble students of our intuition. I mean this in two ways. One is our resistance to taking our own medicine. We freely hand out intuitive guidance but sit in our blindspots, unwilling to offer ourselves what we are sharing with others. I've mentioned this aspect in previous chapters because it is pervasive. The second way we are spiritually fragile regarding humility is our failure to train and evolve our intuition. Intuition is innate within us, but if we intend to work with it in our service, professionally or in any other way, then we have a responsibility to develop it. When we fail to do this, we are in our ego, acting as if intuition is a gift and must not be questioned.

One of my earliest intuition teachers was a jovial Frenchman, who supported me to train my intuition through weekly circles. We would gather on a Wednesday evening in a small room above a shop. All of the students would take turns standing at the front of the room and working the muscle of our intuition by channelling for the group as a whole or someone specifically in the group. Each circle would inevitably end with him channelling for us. I do not discount how much I gained from my time as his student. But the time came when I recognised he had taken my intuition training as far as possible. I was also increasingly uncomfortable with the blurred boundaries between our professional and personal relationships. We worked for a time in the same place, and I found that he would often go into teacher or channel mode when we were not in the learning environment and sometimes share in public, private information revealed in the sanctity of the circle. This was something I observed occurring with a number of his students.

One day I went to his home to tell him that my time as his student was over. I expressed my gratitude and let him know that I wanted more explicit boundaries between us. Almost instantly, he went into 'channelling' mode. Instead of talking to me about my decision, he began to 'channel' his guide, Archangel Michael, who advised me of how wrong my decision was. This went on for some time and eventually I cut him off and departed. I knew exactly what was happening. This man was attempting to make me doubt myself by bringing in a 'higher authority'. If I wasn't going to listen to the man then I would have to listen to the guide. But I knew too much by then to buy into this, and my primary intuition alarm bells were going off. I was not safe in this space anymore. He was no longer my teacher. His lack of humility, and his rejection of my own intuitive knowing, is a dark aspect of this work. Just because it is 'intuition' doesn't mean it isn't being utilised in an abusive or manipulative way.

We live in a time of chaos. Human consciousness is going through an enormous upleveling process, and those who can lead must. We must be prepared, as the great mystic Ken Wilber invites us, to *shake the spiritual tree*[22]. It is not enough for us to attain inner peace for ourselves. It is not enough for us to have our pleasant little lives and comfort/familiar zones. We must take ourselves out into the world and offer those still in the darkness what we have understood. And part of that is the responsibility to commit to ongoing development of our highest form of intelligence. The only teacher I trust is the one who never stops being the student. To be the teacher is to be the demonstration of our faith. If we are offering intuitive advice, are we taking that advice ourselves? Our service is always our medicine. Be the first recipient and student of your words.

## Intention and attention

To illustrate further what falls into the trinket and superstitions, here's an incomplete inventory. *Channelled codes from those with a special gift that activate something in us, signs like pink feathers, numbers appearing, in a particular order, magical portal (man-made) calendar dates, a special gift for channelling ascended energies, communing with fairies, spirit guides, dead people, and releasing on a full moon above any other day.* It is all just consciousness communicating with itself, and that consciousness is God. Placing our attention on

---

22 Ken Wilber, *One Taste*, 1999. The full quote is as follows, 'And therefore, all of those for whom authentic transformation has deeply unseated their souls must, I believe, wrestle with the profound moral obligation to shout from the heart—perhaps quietly and gently, with tears of reluctance; perhaps with fierce fire and angry wisdom; perhaps with slow and careful analysis; perhaps by unshakable public example—but authentically always and absolutely carries a demand and duty: you must speak out, to the best of your ability, and shake the spiritual tree, and shine your headlights into the eyes of the complacent. You must let that radical realization rumble through your veins and rattle those around you'.

these things should be a step towards oneness, not a cause to stay in separation.

What's the antidote? Do we have to give up all our crystals? Not all. But we must engage with them honestly, intentionally and consciously.

Everything I see is innocent when I intend to see as God sees, and I focus on that desire without wavering. I do not have to forgo anything, although I just as quickly recognise that I do not need anything. What motivates my desire for that thing, that behaviour, that belief? Is it bringing me closer to God or further away?

Look at it this way: the law that *all is one* is as true on the earthly plane as it is in the invisible realms. Yet most of us do not walk around identifying everyone we see as an innate aspect of ourselves. We are seven billion faces of one energy. Angels, guides, crystals, sage, places, practices, prayers, deities and so on are all individuated expressions of one divine essential energy or truth. God. Communication with God, or superconsciousness, is not something we reach *out* for. We are reaching inwards *into* superconsciousness. As above, so below. As within, so without. When we meet the ascended masters or animal spirits or place crystals on our altar, whether we know it or not, we intend to go to God. God is everything. God is overcoming the belief in separation. God is unified consciousness. What does this mean in real terms?

It means we stop saying things that spiritual people say all the time without realising what they are doing,

*Spirit guided me to do…*

*My angels say…*

*I'm getting a download…*

There is simply no need for any of that kind of language when we know the true nature of God. There is nothing that is not of God. When we say that we connect to our intuition, we falsely suggest that we are sometimes *not* connected to our intuition. Our intuition is simply us remembering we are God. Our God Consciousness is all that we are. Everything else is a faulty split or division in that consciousness. The ego attempts to separate us from what we are, for the ego is the part of us that believes it is separate from God. God is the yearning in our souls to unite with what we indeed are, our ceaseless longing to become whole.

Contemporary spiritual teacher, Byron Katie, tells this story of communicating with her 'guide', the lady, at a challenging time in her life after she woke up to her God nature:

What I have come to know is that I projected the lady... like a movie ... as a result of painful limitations I was experiencing in this dimension. We give ourselves exactly what we need. We supply our own medicine ... Today I don't wait for angels. I am always the angel I have been awaiting, and so are you. It's not out there, it's in here ... some people would project Christ, others Krishna ... I projected a fat lady with a bun on her head wearing a paisley dress – that's who I could trust. Now I trust all. I woke up knowing that God is everything ... There is no exception in my experience[23].

If we privilege the personality of the guide, then we believe in separation. If we respond to our guides archetypally, their meaning and role in our lives are suddenly apparent. Why would I be so drawn to Jesus, the greatest healer the world has ever known? It has nothing to do with Jesus Christ in the literal

---

23 Dan Millman & Doug Childers, *Bridge Between Worlds*, 2009.

sense and everything to do with what Jesus symbolically represents. The qualities embodied by the Christ Consciousness are qualities I aspire to embody. The archetype is the framework around which I can build my own consciousness. Is Jesus any less real to me because I am conjuring that energy within me? No, he is more real, for I have overcome my faulty belief in separation. Communication with our nonlocal guides in this way can be thought of as a form of consciousness encoding. We are up-levelling our consciousness by holding our intention and attention on the consciousness of what we can become within our hearts and minds. We are showing our consciousness how we want it to behave. This is very liberating. Where we place our attention with intention, we create *the* meaning. Then we live that meaning. Remembering, this is happening at the individual and collective level. Why do I feel agitated by the full moon? Because there is a collective belief around it that I am communicating with.

## A note on archetypes

Archetypes are patterns of energy that repeat. They are part of us all, contained within the collective unconscious. These patterns are witnessed many times before being named. They support us to see through form to formlessness. They have shared meaning in our collective consciousness. This is why full moons may be particularly potent for us. There is a collective shared meaning.

On archetypes, the great contemporary mystic Caroline Myss states, 'Archetypes are everywhere. We live and breathe in an archetypal universe. Every relationship we have is an archetypal connection, even with our children, beginning with the primal Mother-Child bond. Every event in society is a creation of our collective archetypal energies. Nothing, not war or peace, not disasters or global events, just "happen." We are participants in everything. We are co-creators of the events unfolding in this world, but the means through which we "co-create" is not our "will power." Co-creation occurs through our archetypal patterns and the deep-rooted stories and beliefs we cling to that are rooted in our archetypes.[24,]

This is why we may argue that using the full moon to release or Archangel Gabriel to cut cords of 'negative' energy or popping crystals in our bra does not impede unity consciousness. We may perceive them as sacred and get closer to our God nature. To an extent, this may be true. But the answer is always to look at our *intention* in using those things. We are so often in a habituated response, unconsciously going through the motions or fulfilling superstitions that we are afraid will 'curse us' in one form or another if we don't. Our crystals will have bad energy if we don't put them out under the full moon. Neither crystals nor the full moon exist except as archetypal patterns of energy and create our reality only through our belief in them, not as objects in and of themselves.

When it comes to the many faces of God, identifying with the archetype rather than a specific historical figure, angel, master, guide etc., allows us to stay out of dogma and preconceived ideas that we may have about the 'personality' we are connecting to. I am much more interested in our connection to the unlimited consciousness that pervades everything, that is us. Individuating divine consciousness into the different kinds of divine support is exciting as it allows us

---

24 Accessed at: https://www.myss.com/cmed/online-institute/series/archetypes-everywhere/

to connect intimately with this energy. If we are moving towards healing our minds of the wounded belief in separateness, then ultimately, I want us to remember: that which we are communicating with is us. It is vibrating at a higher frequency than us simply because it doesn't have to hold form together in the way we do. Higher frequency = less density.

All consciousness is communicating. We can pay attention to this at any time, although it won't always be to get information. Instead, this communion with the invisible consciousness is a direct reminder of the unifying energy that moves through all of us, that *is* us. If it works better for us, go straight to God. Our nonlocal guides are simply showing up in accordance with our beliefs about them. So how do we ensure the highest level of communication with God? Do the damn work.

## Do the damn work

*You Are Not An Empath.*
Actually, we all are. Yet, just because I say that there is nothing unique about being highly sensitive and empathic doesn't mean we shouldn't care deeply about this part of ourselves. We should normalise attending to the biological truth of what we are. How do we do this? Our humanity is beautiful and wild and needs us to show up to it in all its fullness. It's ok that being highly sensitive and empathic doesn't make us special. It's time to make this normal. These are basic human needs, not special spiritual rarities. We are One. We all need these things. Let's get over ourselves, so we can create a reality that works for the greatest good, instead of ghettoising ourselves with our

imaginary 'spiritual' fragility. My energetic sensitivity is a superpower, not a deficiency. But like all great superpowers, it needs me to tend to it with care. The greatest way to tend to ourselves is through devotion.

We must ask ourselves these questions;

*How deep is my devotion? How active is my faith? Do I have a deep, enduring and abiding practice that buoys me up to weather the storms of life, which will keep coming by the way, regardless of how devoted I am, because spirituality is not insurance against the difficult events of life?*

If we practise our faith with devotion, it will guard against constant disappointment. We will become deeply trusting of life. An excellent way to gauge the depth of our spirituality is to look at what we do in the privacy of our own life when no one is looking. Devotion prepares us for whatever life presents, including the shocking discovery that we have been spiritually fragile and creating more separation consciousness. No matter how 'good' we think we are, we have a divine responsibility to get as uncomfortable as hell to serve the greater good by the right of our birth. To be free enough to pursue the soul's awakening is a privilege not to be squandered.

We do this by becoming finely tuned for superconsciousness. Why is this uncomfortable? We are moving from the 'magic bullet' mentality, wherein something outside of us will provide the way, to the truth that we must sweat for God. If our body's addicted to being busy, addicted to stress, fear, and anxiety, the second we sit with ourselves, we're going to go into a state of panic. Or we're going to start imagining that our house is burning down, or there's something wrong with one of our kids. As we learned in the previous chapter, it takes time to disarm and regulate.

The commitment to live in a way that supports the increase of our innate intuition to the level of Intuitive Intelligence is an essential and often missed phase in the process. That's because it requires consistency, practice and more practice, and we desperately want the easy way out. We don't want to take the time necessary to train our consciousness over years and even decades. We want a quick fix. The answer is always within. The following practices, used daily with intention and attention, will support increased access to superconsciousness:

- Stillness, silence and solitude
- Meeting our subconscious fear with conscious intent
- Being conscious and intentional in all our actions
- Doing at least one thing in holy service
- Reading a sacred text
- Find pleasure in the mundane chores by becoming fully present as you do
- Laugh
- Express appreciation
- Alter your vibration at will by cultivating a feeling state disproportionate to evidence.

This list is by no means exhaustive, but it is enough, to begin with. If practised with dedication, it creates self-reliance. Nothing on this list requires us to spend money, change location, seek anything outside of us. It needs humility to change our lives to make all of these elements possible. We so often say we are willing but are we really? If we have to get uncomfortable, will we stay the course? We commonly say one thing, but our actions do the opposite.

# The lies that we tell ourselves

To develop our intuition and live in a spiritually mature relationship with all four phases of our intuition, we have to be willing to cultivate a life that allows us to access our intuition. There are three key ingredients as mentioned at the top of the list in the previous section — stillness, silence, and solitude. Why do these qualities matter so much? Because they tell us the truth faster than anything else.

Very often, we'll say,

*I can't hear my intuition.*

And what we mean is,

*As I was running from dropping my kids off to going to the supermarket, to chasing clients, to picking them up again, to taking them to after school activities, to making dinner, I didn't have any moments of full conscious realisation of my intuition, because I had no moments of full consciousness. I was on autopilot. I was running.*

Most of us say,

*I want more intuition.*

But what would we be willing to change? What would we change in our day? What would we have to say no to find that stillness? I don't mean just flopping in a chair. I mean intentional stillness, bringing the body into devotion through meditation, or whatever it is for us. Silence, not just because the TV is not on. Intentional silence where we are eliminating all of that external noise. Solitude, not just because no one was home, but because we made an active choice to shut the door, and lock it, and tell everyone on the other side of it,

*I am not available right now.*

What we're really talking about is, are we willing to give time to our mystic and let our mystical self have time every day? Now we may say,

*Oh yeah, but I meditate. And I go to yoga.*

But if we aren't doing that every day with intentionality and in a devoted way, then it's unlikely that we're going to create the conditions in our life where we can move into that surrender intuition. It requires intention and attention. But we pretend we are too busy because the most challenging thing about opening to our intuition is that we have to act upon it. It's much easier to say,

*I don't know what my intuition is saying*

In truth, we are saying,

*I really don't want to know what my intuition is saying.*

This is because we do not want to take responsibility for the action it's asking us to take.

If we create the conditions where that knowledge becomes absolute certainty, we have to take responsibility and take action. Because if we don't, we're breaking the cosmic laws. To ask for more intuition, go towards increasing our intuition, and then not act on our intuition is breaking the law. We're acting in bad faith. We wanted our intuition, but it turns out we just wanted an easy ride.

When our intuition says,

*You have to stop eating that way. You have to stop living that way. You have to stop abusing yourself or that other person,*

We say,

*But then I'd have to be disapproved of. I can't risk that.*

We'd prefer to live lives that are a lie a lot of the time. Lying to ourselves and lying to others. So we're saying,

*I want more intuition. I want more intuition.*

But what we mean is,

*I want more of the party trick where I get to predict someone else's future, or I can see your aura. Or I can find a parking spot.*

We want more comfort. But to live in intuitive intelligence is to say,

*I want to live in a flow state with a God mind all of the time and to be in that state of truth.*

That means we have to *live* that state of truth. Because if we keep asking to see the truth, and then we keep living a lie, we're then at war with ourselves. When we're at war with ourselves, we break down the communication channel between ourselves and God. Intuition is our highest form of intelligence. We must be humble enough to train for it. If we want to be masterful at anything, we've got to show up. We've got to do the damn work. We've got to commit.

Why is it so different with our intuition? It isn't, but the new age spin has brainwashed us — that it's outside of us, that it's a gift, that we can buy our way into more of it with the crystal or the light or the special elixir. Do the damn work. Stillness. Silence. Solitude. Create a life that is congruent with our desire to increase our intuition. It's not a special gift. But it does have special conditions. We must show our intuition respect because it connects us to the greatest power we have — the capacity to see through the illusion to truth.

## Looking through the illusion

Intuitive Intelligence brings the ability to see both the local plane and the nonlocal plane concurrently. To be able to see the material plane through the plane of pure consciousness is, in my opinion, the most tremendous power we have, the most significant action we can take to move the world beyond the current state of affairs. This is not about cultivating a sight that takes us beyond the world and bypasses the current reality, but instead bringing us into a deep state of compassionate action – to see the failures and flaws in privileging the material plane. The overlaps, and more importantly, the disconnections of holding two contrary states of sight simultaneously, allow us to take action at the level of form, which is informed by the spiritual or energy dimension first. We privilege our spiritual nature first as a result. What we want from this level powerfully contradicts what we want at the level of form. In other words, to cultivate spiritual sight is to surrender the ego-identified self and to step into a bigger vision of who and what we are. It is to cultivate God Consciousness. Because contemporary spirituality tells us that we are on the right track when we are focussed simply on using our spirituality to enhance the material plane, we have only seen through *form to formlessness*. What happens if we put our spiritual sight first?

There is no simple truth of reality. The world's status quo wants us to believe that things are simply the way they are. Yet as we open to and privilege our spiritual sight, we can see through this illusion to a greater reality, a higher truth, one in which we do not seek our advantage to the disadvantage of another. Spiritual sight, the coexistence of the mundane and the spiritual, at the very least, keeps us uncomfortable enough to ask why things are the way they are and what else is possible.

The development of spiritual sight alongside our ordinary sight is key to developing a new paradigm of consciousness. If we use our spiritual sight to bypass, overlook, or opt-out of the current status of the world, we are causing more harm than good. We are causing as much harm as when we use the cultivation of spiritual sight simply to make the local reality better. Our spirituality is not meant to help us increase the nightmare of separation, to build more layers into the illusion. Our spiritual sight is our return to the One Mind, and the coexistence of both human and divine sight gives us the ultimate power to make change for all humanity. This is why we wake up. This is how we free ourselves and all consciousness from the dream.

## Gilded Cages

In a powerful guided journey a few years ago, I heard the words,

*You gilded your cages with gold and thought you had bought your freedom.*

Long after the meditation was over, I could not shake these words from my consciousness. I didn't want to. This is a metaphor for what we have done with our spiritual tools and intuition for such a long time. When I look around at the world, I can understand why this is the provocation I needed to hear. We've been using our spiritual tools for anything other than for awakening. We're in prisons of our own making. We're in a prison that we've manufactured in the dream of Earth School, and we've painted it with all the luxuries that we could manufacture through the 'law of attraction' and using our spiritual tools to get our ego's needs met. Getting a bigger house, bigger TV, more stuff, a partner, and a sense of security in a dream is just a paradox in itself. Now we're looking around and realising that we are all still in the cages no matter how pretty we made them. And nobody is free.

It's time to understand what freedom truly is. Spiritual freedom has never been about how many holidays we get to go on a year, how many spiritual books we buy, how many programs we invest in, how many things we can give to our kids, or how much private education we can afford. These are the nightmares that we have substituted for our soul's longing. Superconscious intuition is asking us now to recognise that those things were never going to meet our needs. This is our time to see how deep we are willing to go to get past our addiction to the dream. It will take a while because these things are addictions to us. Are we ready to go beyond our ego's addictions to get those needs met, those things that feel like needs but never were and will never satisfy our longing? Every wealthy person who's ever made it to the top of the pile has told us that the things that we're seeking will not bring us happiness. Yet we still think that if we get all our physical security met, somehow we're going to find what we want. It is not okay anymore for us to sit in that paradigm. The world is melting away all of the illusion.

We cannot control the dream. We cannot manipulate a dream. We might be able to do it temporarily, but ultimately the dream will win. The dream as a metaphor for life is not a new idea. It is written about in ancient sacred texts. Plato wrote about it as the allegory of the cave. The people watch shadows projected on the wall from objects passing in front of a fire behind them and give names to these shadows. The shadows are the prisoners' reality but are not accurate representations of the real world. The shadows represent the fragment of reality that we can normally perceive through our senses. In the allegory, one prisoner is freed, and slowly his eyes adjust to the light of the sun, and he can see the truth. He returns to the cave to attempt to free others. We're waking up to the truth that we are in these cages, in caves watching shadows, and thinking it is life, at this level of consciousness. Our job is to attain freedom from all limiting beliefs. That is how we attain freedom for all. Our task is to set one another free. It is time to open the door to the gilded cage and walk out into the light of truth. How do we do this? We seek only to meet ourselves as God.

## Don't make intuition yet another trinket

The great French astrophysicist, Jacques Vallée, says that the dimensions of time and space don't truly exist. Still, their function is to allow us to know ourselves, to let our consciousness traverse time and space, which are imaginary constructs. These constructs exist so that we can learn more about ourselves[25]. That's why we have this construct of intuition, but please don't get caught up in it because it serves a purpose, just as time and space are serving a purpose. That purpose is for us to know ourselves.

I don't care how we do it. I don't care how we go and meet ourselves as God, but by golly, we must make that our life purpose because that is the work of this life. And if for one moment we get caught up in the belief that something else is

---

25 Accessed at: https://youtu.be/S9pR0gfil_0

157

the purpose, then we'll just have to keep coming back again and again and again until we figure it out. *Know thyself, and you will know the mysteries of the gods and of the universe*[26]. That is it. To know ourselves is to know that we are God and that there is nothing outside of our capacity. What happens, though, when we come to that realisation, that recognition, we desire then is to be with that superconsciousness as much as possible simply. That's why intuition matters, but only as a step on the path — intuition matters as a way into our infinite nature.

When we get too caught up in the idea of intuition as the endpoint, or a special magic tool that we want to get good at, we're humanising our spiritual superpower. It's about liberating ourselves from the idea that we would pursue intuition in isolation. To pursue the tools of intuition, trying and getting good at working with any of the trinkets and superstitions of intuition, is breaking the cosmic laws. Ultimately we want to need our intuition no longer. That's such a shift in our consciousness that it may take a little while to make peace with it. Please be with the process. The future of intuition is the end of the need for intuition; it's a redundancy.

As I said before, intuition is just a symptom of overcoming the belief in separation. Its primary premise is,

*I am a divine piece of a benevolent superconsciousness that always serves my awakening.*

---

26 The origin of this saying is disputed. It was inscribed at the Temple of Apollo at Delphi. But according to Jacqueline Madison, '"Man Know Thyself " is an Ancient African phrase that was written above each temple and lodge serving as academic learning centers in Ancient Africa (Akebulan the mother of mankind which is the continents original name Africa is the name given the continent by Europeans. This phrase which has been the foundation of Ancient Africa/Akebulan represents a thorough and complete education system misnomered as a mystery system. It was in Africa thousands of years prior to Greek, Roman, Persian, Chinese or any other ethnic groups entered Africa to study there. It was the Greeks who began their long period of studies in the Ancient African learning centers that is why they were able to plagiarize many of the Ancient texts and systems.' Accessed at: https://www.quora.com/Was-know-thyself-a-quote-by-Socrates

We must practice rigorously to embody this. We have to work hard to overcome the habit of believing that we are separate and finite. All of the practices of intuition development should help us overcome that belief in separation. We need to practice this because everything we see around us tells us what success looks like and feels like is very different from what our soul is here to do.

## Spiritual fierceness

Several recent studies of spiritual seekers concluded that it is not the quieting of the ego, but the increase in spiritual self-worth, that supports our awakening the most[27]. The primary foundation stone of Intuitive Intelligence is spiritual fierceness. To commit to seeing ourselves as God is the first step of activating our intuition. This is spiritual self-worth. These are great questions to increase self-worth,

*What could I do to start the process of beginning to trust myself? What will I do as fearful thoughts arise that try to tell me that I can't trust myself or if someone's opinion of me derails me? How can I navigate myself back to a relationship with myself that is not built on doubt?*

Doubt is the enemy of intuition, and that's why we go and pay money for other people to tell us the answers to our life. We want to abdicate responsibility for the power that we have. But that power is, as we've now heard, God's power, and it's not to be denied and can't be denied. We can try to give our power away, but it ends up very much that we live a half-life and have to be in a state of denial. Denial is a tough state of being for us to sustain. Anyone who's lived in denial will know what I'm

---

27 Scott Barry Kaufman, 2021 Accessed at: https://www.scientificamerican.com/article/the-science-of-spiritual-narcissism/

talking about. It takes a ton of energy to stay in denial when everything inside of us is screaming the truth. To live in that state where we sit in denial requires so much force that we will often make ourselves very unwell, mentally or physically or spiritually. We will be in disordered relationships. We will be in a state of co-dependence with the people around us because we have to make bigger and bigger the illusion of the ego to try and sustain that denial. Intuitive Intelligence is a deep state of being beyond the question. There's no need to ask a question. There is no question to be asked because it is an embodied state. It's a fully present state. It's a state where we are one with the temple of this human life. It's not our enemy. And it's showing us, supporting us to awaken to that state of absolute knowing.

It will become a flow state, where we are simply moving through the world with that absolute sense of spiritual fierceness. It's only when that flow state disappears, and we feel a little bit uncomfortable or disordered, or it feels like things have just gone a little bit awry, that we recognise that we've stepped out of living in communion with superconsciousness. Intuitive Intelligence is learning how to have that relationship with the Superconscious Mind, and spiritual fierceness is the heat that makes it happen. That connection is a vibrational frequency connection that goes beyond what is seen with the physical eyes, and therefore we forget about it. We're lazy because we have not wedded ourselves to our spiritual fierceness, and our spiritual self-esteem has not risen to the point where we default to that.

Intuitive Intelligence is choosing to default to our superconscious sight. It means breaking the habits and addictions to thinking like a human. It means breaking the habits and addictions to the way that the ego wants to keep us in a low vibrational state, making it much harder to access these effortless states for receiving the communication of the Superconscious Mind. We need to recognise that we cannot sit in our fear and spiritual *floppiness* and expect it to be effortless to live in that flow state. We have to do the work to show up to the state of being or the vibration that will allow us to connect to that communion most efficiently.

That requires putting down all of that doubt, which is a process. It's not a fixed endpoint. The process is not linear. To awaken our Intuitive Intelligence, we must not be defeated because we have a good day, and then we have a series of bad days before we have the next good day. I was on a retreat recently with a group, and every morning we gathered in early morning meditation. Every person there would say, some days their practice was,

*I am owning this meditation game. I'm kicking all the goals.*

Other days it's like,

*Ah! Can my brain stop with the analysis just for a minute?*

But they didn't stop attending. That's not a reason to not show up the next day. That's the reason we should show up the next day because it simply means that the process of awakening to that part of us is still ongoing. Living in the flow state of Intuitive Intelligence does not mean that it is easy. It simply means that we have changed our perception of our life events. We see everything in service to our awakening rather than it being a series of things happening to us to derail us from our spiritual paths. Very often in our spiritual journey, as we begin, we'll put down our practices every time life gets busy. It's the first thing we do. When things get complicated, we'll just stop meditating. We'll stop doing our devotion. We'll stop doing prayer. We stop asking God for help. We'll stop doing our visioning, and we'll say,

*Oh, because life's too big right now.*

That's the point of our practices. Our devotion and spiritual fierceness are the things that can navigate us through the difficult times of our lives. They are not the things that we show up to try and prevent difficult things from happening to us. This is such a misnomer about the idea of spirituality generally, but the role of intuition is not to help us avoid life. It's not to give us the heads up to not go that direction because that person's going to be mean to us, and we'll feel bad about ourselves for the rest of the day. It's to afford us a change of perception, and that's what spiritual fierceness is. It's changing our minds about ourselves so that we no longer see our reality as the enemy. We will be able to sit in a flow state if we can change our perception of ourselves and no longer feel like victims of our reality. This requires spiritual fierceness.

## Living in service

I want us to progress the conversation about intuition to be about collective good, not personal gain. So that it is motivated by the question,

*How may I be of service?*

instead of,

*What can I get?*

As a global consciousness, we will no longer sit in the dream, the nightmare of separation when this happens. We will no longer perpetuate the acts of violence against one another and the earth because we will be embodying the inherent interconnectedness of all life. We will acknowledge, first and foremost, our life is service.

The difference between intuition as just a thing that we do because we're a bit scared about choosing our future versus Intuitive Intelligence is that we don't ever turn off our Intuitive Intelligence. You don't put it down. You don't have to do something to turn it on and turn it off. It is us in partnership with God, and we don't want to turn that off, not ever. You want to be in that relationship all of the time because it's the better, more magnificent part of us. It is us. Intuitive Intelligence exists on the other side of belief, and belief is what keeps us in prison. And every time a thought arises in us, it's our job to choose whether we follow where that belief is trying to take us. The more we train ourselves to stay present and the more we train ourselves to be spiritually fierce, we will not go with every negative self-belief. We will no longer be self-obsessed.

It begins with choosing to follow that higher part of ourselves, even though we have no freaking idea where that will take us. The future of intuition is that we no longer live as though our little piece of the world, our little bit of happiness, and just the people we gave birth to are what matters. It is the recognition that as pure vibration, as pure consciousness, we are here in service to that greater good. Because there is only one consciousness. There is only one of us here. The future of intuition is that we no longer even talk about intuition. We are simply present to our superconsciousness, breath by breath, moment by moment, and that we do not doubt that we are worthy of having that communion and that communion is with ALL for ALL.

# PART THREE: THE REVOLUTION

*Dear God,*
*Expand my sacred vision so that I may bear witness to the full*
*expression of your plan for me.*
*Let me be moved beyond my limited perception of myself so*
*that I may inherit the unlimited truth of what I AM.*
*And so it is.*
*And it is so.*

# Chapter 8

# Creating Space

*"You are so powerful that when you think you're not, you're not"*.

— *Unknown*

A few years ago, I realised with some discomfort that I'd let my teachings allow people to sit inside the limited and finite paradigm. That's the opposite of everything that I want. I witnessed such a rise in the holding space movement that I wondered if I should also be offering the option to not move beyond the dysregulation that we all carry from individual experience and due to being born into a human experience. Holding space is defined as witnessing and validating someone's emotional state whilst also being present to our own. This is vital work. Presence is the holy grail of spiritual awakening, and we simply cannot do anything, not meditate or awaken our Intuitive Intelligence without it. I've had people fight me,

*How dare you try to take my anxiety from me? How dare you tell me what I'm feeling or that I don't have to feel this fear?*

My response is,

*Actually, you do. I'm telling you the opposite. I want you to feel it. I want you to be unafraid to feel it because what's causing you the suffering is your war with truth. Your truth is right now; I am in fear. My life feels heavy and burdensome. I don't know how to do this on my own. And I need you to get down on your knees with that truth. I don't want you to pretend anymore, stop arguing. This is where you're at.*

It's only there in that surrender that we open to the change that is waiting to rush in to serve us. That is the end of the war with the self. That's where we can open to bliss. Knowing how to work with fear in this way for ourselves and those we serve is a remarkable blessing. But it may not make us popular. I recall an experience on a retreat in the jungle in Bali a few years ago. I facilitated a session where we moved through the ARC process outlined in Chapter Six. It was a profound group experience, and under the light of the full moon, I could sense how deep the group had gone in changing their state of being. The group shared their personal experiences of the process as we moved around the circle. We were winding down, preparing to head off to our rooms for sleep. It was the turn of the final person in the group to share, and before she spoke a word, I could feel her seething rage. She spoke calmly, but her words were angry. She accused me of undermining her feelings, belittling her trauma and negating her pain. She rejected the process outright. I had tried to take her pain from her, she stated. She accused me of behaving dangerously and unethically. I was tired; my defences were down after such a heart-opening experience. I was unprepared for her rage, and I confess, I took it personally. It was a humbling and uncomfortable experience, and I took the rest of the week-long retreat to reflect on my actions. What I came to understand is this.

Holding space is a necessary first step to true healing, no matter how we define healing. But along with this rise in the holding space movement, there is an accompanying belief that *this is it*. There is no greater goal than to become present to the shit show of our lives or whatever repressed trauma is arising. Caroline Myss calls this *woundology*[28]. Self-awareness of our trauma to the extent that we define ourselves by it and defend our right to build our identity around our wounds. But if I am witnessing you from a place of compassion, which is all I can do if I have done the deep work, then I see you as God sees you. I am creating the space for you to see yourself that way too. Self-awareness isn't the end goal. Self-realisation is. And that is defined as the fulfilment of one's potential. Our potential in this life is to know ourselves as what we are, which is God. Intuition is the path to that truth. I realised then that I wasn't on board with holding space. I am interested in *creating space*. The space I create is of compassion,

*I see you as God sees you, and I create the space for you to see that too. No matter what has happened to you or what you have done to others, you are worthy of knowing yourself as God — infinite, unlimited, holy and divine. Live from that place. Love from that place. Heal from that place.*

What I teach is not everybody's cup of tea because I don't hold space for littleness. Creating space creates a new reality. Holding space maintains the status quo, and it should only be the first step on the path. Then, we meet our fear. Then we get to it, creating the conditions for changing that fear to love. How

---

28 From *Why people don't heal and how they can*, 1998.

do we do that? How do we meet our infinite power? To be witnessed in our power, connection, and remembrance of self is the way, and it is a rare and precious wonder. It can move mountains and melt away lifetimes of fear. All fear is one fear. I implore us not to make a bedfellow of fear. We must be curious and willing to explore fear knowing that it contains the keys to our awakening. And on the other side is power. True, abiding, all-encompassing, grace infilled power.

Intuition is a step on that path. If we want to connect to the idea that we're God, we have to focus on communion with the God Mind to the exclusion of all else, because our human identity keeps us believing that we're separate. Intuitive Intelligence is the state of being in which we can meet our unlimited power. From observing the holding space movement, I understood that many of us are afraid of our power. That will often come down to the fact that we are fearful of God. Why are we afraid of God? Why are we holding space for littleness?

It comes down to this. We are responding to the dream as though it is real. We are holding space for the dream instead of creating the dream. Even though everything we read and study tells us that we are generating the dream, we continue to do that. Why do we keep behaving as though this dream is primary and precedes us? Consciousness precedes matter. I ask myself whenever I feel less than superconscious,

*Why am I sitting inside a dream that is less than my infinite, unlimited self? Why am I behaving in accordance with a limited perception of reality?*

Instead of making the dream behave itself, what if I simply zoom out and remember my Superconscious nature, which is the generator of reality? The cosmos is being generated in response to our individual and our collective consciousness.

This was my challenge when I realised that I'd been indulging people's fears inside of the dream. The way that I sought to change that was to change my behaviour. I'm a teacher. Teaching is demonstrating. Teaching isn't me telling you things and not doing those things for myself.

## Holy Power

I remember vividly the moment I realised that it was time to shift the focus of the Institute's work from intuition development to sacred leadership. The depth of our connection to our intuition indicates the depth of our connection to our holy power. It was becoming increasingly unavoidable to acknowledge I was training holy leaders! And I didn't want to avoid that. I wanted to run towards it. I knew this to be true because I witnessed those I served running from their power just as they were about to step into it. Holy power is the only power that we privilege in our superconscious state, but we often mistake it for egoic power because the latter is the kind of power we see in the world. How do we make peace with the idea that we are all-powerful, for this is what it comes down to? People get uncomfortable with me talking about them as God because what I'm saying is,

*You are all-powerful. There is nothing stopping you from fully expressing your optimised self, which is God, which is infinite, unlimited consciousness.*

Pursuing the path of sacred leadership is the opposite of egoic because it finally admits the truth of what we are, which is God, and that is humility itself. It's a return to love. The denial is when we enter into false humility; and egoic ideas of leadership that make us believe we are special and different from others. So I watched student after student dull themselves down. They let themselves be comfortable with a small vision of themself and then created the conditions to disempower themselves. Then they would say things like,

*Well, this is all I'm capable of right now, Ricci-Jane. I've got things going on in my life right now. This drama is happening for me right now, Ricci-Jane.*

Instead of seeing themselves as the creator of that reality, they were responding to reality as though it were primary and stayed wedded to the little vision of themselves. Let me be clear here. I am not speaking about the wealth or business success they attained. I am talking about the perception and the power they have to change the world as vibrational beings. I've had students hit one roadblock, one challenge, and crumble. They were waiting for an excuse in the dream to stay small energetically. I have witnessed others face the most terrifying life situations, such as a critically ill child or the death of a partner, and never consider for a moment that this would make them less glorious. If we're sitting in a tiny vision of our life because we're terrified of our power, this is the day that I call us all out, and I ask us to stop comforting ourselves with the known. We are so terrified of our power we will accept less than we are worth, believing that this kind of pseudo-spiritual humility is how we are being more godly.

*If I don't hold a big vision for my life, then I'm just being humble, and it's okay for me, and all I want to do is be here and be comfortable.*

What we're saying is,

*I'm terrified. I am terrified of meeting myself as that which I truly am. I'm terrified of bringing that into the world because what if people don't like me?*

172

People often don't like me, or they'll like me for a while, and as soon as they get close to meeting their infinite nature, they'll find a problem. They'll find a way to blame the messenger. That's okay because it's not my job to be liked. If someone puts me on a pedestal, it's often because they've never met their fierce power before, so they think I'm the source of it. When they start to get close to that power within and realise that it is them, they panic. Not consciously, but subconsciously. They get to the truth, and the ego doesn't want that. So they look for an excuse. As the mirror to the power within them, the effort is to stop me shining, so they don't have to go all the way through to their God power. My actions, my words, my teachings, whatever it is they land on, are the reason they couldn't go further. They push me off the pedestal and create emotional chaos to avoid meeting themselves. Then they'll placate themselves with a dulled down version of what is possible for them. They stay in the shallow end of intuition and play in the trinkets. The spiritual comfort/familiar zone. The spiritualised ego. The self-sabotage is a mighty archetypal pattern I have seen so many times.

The world so needs us in our superconsciousness, and there is nothing in the pseudo-spiritual work, the wellness industry, mindset or personal development that will get us there. There's nothing in that which will change the world as we know it. The paradigm we need to occupy is,

*I am God. I am unlimited power, and I am ready to use that truth to serve the world. My prayer is, Dear God, let my life be a demonstration of your power.*

It's okay to be disliked. It's okay to be disapproved of, and we can still thrive. I am living proof of that because there are many who desire to make me the enemy when they meet their power and don't have the spiritual stamina to go all the way. I am still okay. I am still glorious. I'm still excited about my purpose and life because I am here in service to the greatest good, not my ego's satisfaction.

## Spiritually 'comfortable' is a lie

Feeling comfortable isn't a sign of our intuition. As we know by now, it's simply familiarity. That familiarity deceives us into thinking that this ordinary life is what we want. It isn't what we want. That sharp feeling of discomfort shaking us out of our comfort zone – that's our intuition, agitating us awake. Rousing us from the slumber of this waking dream that we're pretending is us living our best lives. Superconscious intuition is like the grain of sand in the oyster. It will reveal itself as the pearl, but we'll have to work for it. We're being called on a grand adventure — the greatest of them all to journey to the very purpose of our lives, which is to meet ourselves as God. But we'll not get much comfort on the path. Just a constant sense of agitation, God Consciousness is nudging us in the right direction. The only direction.

We don't get to choose how we awaken. We wish we did. We buy into all the false spiritual lies, ideas that lead us to believe we can manifest our awakening on our terms. The ego's needs have nothing to do with the purpose of this life. This precious life is laden with purpose. The purpose is to awaken to the truth of what we are. We are asleep. Our holy task is to wake up. But not to wake up to more layers of the dream. To be 'woke' in the dream is still to be asleep. Being awake has nothing to do with getting more invested in this consciousness experiment called life. It is awakening to the reality that this life is a dream. We are the dreamers. Collectively and individually, we must dream better and ultimately awaken. That is the experiment. It is how we set ourselves and all consciousness free. So stop seeking the deeper meaning of the dream.

We see the spoon. We are angry at the spoon. We are in love with the spoon. We are making meaning of the spoon that has nothing to do with the spoon because the spoon doesn't exist. During the Covid-19 pandemic, I was asked what the spiritual meaning of the pandemic was? My response was always the same. The infinite intelligence of this consciousness experiment will arrange everything for the most rapid and efficient awakening. Our only task is to use whatever conditions before us to awaken. Our freedom of choice, our power to 'manifest' is in how we respond. That's it — the infinite uses whatever conditions are provided. So let's provide better conditions. This is how we ease the suffering of the world.

We must choose our response, knowing it is the most powerful action we can take. The decision is irrelevant. We cannot make a wrong choice when choosing from love, not human love but divine love. We must stop being so shocked by the state of the world. We have been spiritualising the ego and calling it an awakening, and the reckoning time has come. It is time for us to get over the idea that our spiritual path should make us more comfortable. The spiritual path is the most radical of them all. It is revolutionary. It is the power that creates reality. The perceived 'sickness' we see in the collective right now reflects how we have used our spirituality like despotic tyrants tending to our ego's wants.

The word sovereign is used a lot in the world right now, usually to indicate that the 'right' choice has been made, according to our sense of right or wrong. There is no right or wrong. Sovereign means to possess ultimate power. And we do, as the dreamers of this dream. But we aren't being sovereign when we play in the illusion. We are being reactionary. We imagine it is all shocking, out of our hands, happening through no fault of our own. We have created this reality together. We have done so by playing God instead of being God. We have empowered our egos, not our souls, and now it is getting real, and we are uncomfortable and outraged.

It is time for collective spiritual maturing. The world reflects our relationship with God, which is really our relationship with ourselves. Immature, egoic, seeking comfort and calling for revolution whilst sitting on our thrones eating cake. Nothing has gone wrong, for nothing can happen in a dream. It is a nightmare that reflects our soul-sickness, and it is necessary. That is our power to change the dream. To recognise it is an illusion and to stop being so invested. To remember it is a necessary illusion, for it is the path to our awakening.

# Chapter 9

# If you Think you need Protection…

*"We have forgotten who and what we are, a transcendental self plugged straight into spirit, speaking with the words of God and shining with the radiance of the Goddess."*

—*Ken Wilber*

I have been taught that I am in danger for so much of my spiritual journey. I'm in danger of things, usually invisible things, although it could be bad people as well. There is an idea that there are hidden forces in the world, on the astral plane, in the 29th dimension outside of my control, that are trying to get me. My only defence is to create some kind of barricade, some kind of fortress around me to seal me off from the dangerous, mad, bad, crazy world out there that's trying to bring me down.

What that does, and what it did in my experience, is contribute to the creation of a whole bunch of superstitions and a whole group of obsessive-compulsive 'spiritual' acts that I felt I had to engage in to be certified spiritual. If I wasn't doing these things, and everybody else was then, I wasn't rocking my spiritual as hard as they were and I was somehow not getting it right.

We often perceive that those who can detect negative thought forms or bad juju or whatever it happens to be are somehow more connected to their intuition than we are — more sensitive. By now, we understand that they simply placed their attention on a lower frequency, possess less spiritual maturity and are more invested in the dream. In naming, identifying and asserting fear, and buying into the illusion of the dream, we cast doubt into people's minds at best, and at worst, we make others feel afraid of their own lives.

We'll see signs everywhere when we realise we create them, not just in the positive. We're not just talking about getting an affirmation we were seeking because we see 11:11 or a feather or a green car. If we have accepted the frequency of a particular belief, we will find evidence for that belief everywhere. We are in a dream, a dream that is a training ground for our consciousness. It responds to our instructions.

Everything that has ever been imagined exists within the dream. We have only one task — deciding which frequency we're going to attune. My mission is to discern which frequency I want to live.

Let's talk about how we energetically protect ourselves if we don't get the right crystal—or seeing a healer, or having a certain number of rituals. Or making sure we've got incense or sage on our altar. Or that the moon's in the right place. Or if our stars are aligned. Or Mercury's not retrograde or any of the other myriad things outside of us to which we give our power.

*I would lead a revolution in consciousness, but unfortunately, Mercury's retrograde this week, so I'm going to sit in just in case my computer breaks.*

Collective consciousness is potent. When enough of us place our attention upon ideas with enough focus over time, we can ensure aspects of reality come to mean what they mean. What have we learned about how possible it is for us to determine the reality that we live? We've discovered three laws. We've learned the three laws that explain the how, what, where, why, and when of determining the reality in which we live.

We're all highly sensitive. We're all barometers of energy, and we're picking up that information all of the time, both through our biology and nonlocal consciousness. There are indeed environments, people and situations that feel heavy; not feeling good about that place, feeling a sense of dread about visiting that particular person because whenever I leave, I'm exhausted, or I have a headache, is a capacity of our regular beingness.

We have all had experiences like this. I am not in any way saying those are not real experiences. We know too much about energy to dismiss those experiences. I want to change our minds about our sense of vulnerability to those people, places, and situations. Instead of going into the world with the paradigm of,

*I must keep myself safe from a mad, bad world full of people draining my energy, energy vampires sucking the life out of me because I am somehow so special and unique that everybody wants to tap into this,*

we could choose a different way of responding, a way that is congruent with the immutable laws. As above so below, as within so without. What did that law teach us? If we are experiencing a fearful world on the outside, we hold fear of the world within us. If I see a mad, bad world, there's a very good chance I'm holding the fear of the mad, bad world inside of me.

179

The greatest protection that we have is to surrender judgement. When we start thinking in terms of frequency instead of binaries of good/bad, light/dark, and so on, we start to recognise that everything is serving us. We can recognise the value of the full spectrum of experience beyond the ego's need to be constantly satisfied or 'safe'. Instead of feeling vulnerable, we can make a better choice, and that better choice is to attune with intention and attention to a different frequency.

That is a choice we make not once. That is a choice we make every damn day through our devotion, practice, and commitment to generating a disproportionate frequency to evidence. We must train ourselves to hold our frequency at a higher vibration. That is ultimately and utterly the only protection we need. Because we are manufacturing our reality, we are then the ones determining the quality of our relationship with the world and generating the world that we inhabit. Now, I don't mean that suddenly the person who feels terrible to hang out with will fall off the face of the earth because they're not a vibrational match for us. Although funnily enough, when we start to hold our vibration at a certain level, people who cannot vibe with us at that level will effortlessly find their way out of our lives.

Our vibration will naturally correspond to its match. Like attracts like. Our task is to hold the highest possible vibration every damn day. Specifically when going into environments that feel challenging. Our job is to double down on generating a high vibrational frequency because we don't need to separate ourselves from that environment. To do so is to break the law. We need to see that environment, person and thought form as ourselves.

We need only to bring ourselves back into wholeness or holiness. Anything that challenges us is an opportunity to find out what's incongruent inside of ourselves. Then we meet that fear to return it to holiness. We do this by raising our consciousness to become a higher vibrational state. We are then protecting ourselves from being dragged down by perceived low vibrational frequencies around us, and we become the blessing. Wherever we go, we allow others to elevate their frequency without even knowing how or why. We just feel so good to be around.

This can be very useful if we understand that, but there are conditions. We all know if we never wash our bodies, we're going to suffer the consequences. Disease and disharmony will occur in the physical body. So it goes with our subtle anatomy. Most of us never learn that we have an energy field that likewise needs care, attention, and cleansing. So we go about in the world suffering because we have not had access to this fundamental information of how to cleanse and purify our energy body, which is simply a function of our biology. Or we have been told, and we ignore it, for myriad reasons, but mostly because it is invisible to our dominant senses, and we just forget.

We all know how to do this. We all do it in different ways. But for me, the most straightforward process to cleanse the subtle body is to hold a high vibrational feeling state every day. The same things allow me to hold a high vibration with ease. So I don't need to do anything fancy. I just need to remember that my energetic field requires me to care for it. That cleansing is to maybe dance for five minutes a day, or listen to a beautiful piece of music, or sit in the sunshine, or hug a tree, meditate, chant, move, sing, eat lightly, rest, retreat, and most importantly, intentionally meet and release fear.

## Entrainment vs resonance

I don't need everything around me to feel great for me to hold a high vibration. At this level of spiritual maturity, it is not about bypassing my feelings. It's not about ignoring reality. It's about recognising that my vibration is not generated based on external data but on that internal state that I can hold at all times, regardless of what is happening in my life. Suppose we think of the old paradigm of energetic protection as excluding aspects of the world that we judge as lesser than. In that case, we are breaking the law and creating more separation nightmares. We are in our right minds if we think about energetic protection as an invitation to oneness.

If I am segregating the world into good or bad, and creating spiritual hierarchies I am in fear that everything out there is dragging me down. I am above them. If I perceive oneness, I am vibing so high I'm dragging everything up. It cannot be any other way. We call this entrainment. The higher vibration will bring others into entrainment with it. When we go into an environment without conscious awareness, we are vulnerable. For example, we visit our auntie, who often brings us down because she is terrified of the world and full of stories of woe. If we don't go in with the conscious awareness that we need to be clear on where our vibration is, we will inevitably come into resonance with her lower frequency.

We go home and feel heavy and sad and loaded down. We take a shower and energetically see the golden light pouring over us, and smudge ourselves with sage, and put crystals in our bra and all of this stuff to bring us back into balance. We might stay in this funk for days. How about we save some time? Instead of coming into resonance with the lowest frequency in a space, how about we entrain the environments and people in that space to our high vibrational setpoint? We commit to

cultivating a vibrational frequency through devotion and practice so that the world does not so easily buffet us around.

We remain aware that there are certain situations in which we want to bring our A-game vibrationally, but we are no longer afraid of the world or the people and things within it. My responsibility is not to segregate myself from the world but rather is to hold the highest possible vibration. I do not do this just for my own 'protection' but for the world's benefit.

## Discernment

The next level of this is discernment. Just because we know how to hold our vibration at a level that can eclipse the shitstorm of other people's emotional chaos and challenging situations and places that don't feel great does not mean that we have to keep going into those environments. We do not have to keep having those relationships that do not feel like a match. We do not need to keep tuning into the lowest level of the astral plane and hanging out with thought-forms. We now have a responsibility to curate a life that reflects the vibration we are holding.

This is discernment. Discernment is hard only because our intuition will often guide us away from things that are not a vibrational match for us anymore, which takes us out of our comfort/familiar zone. It is our holy task not to be afraid to do what God is asking us to do. Harvard-trained theologian Megan

Watterson says, 'Discernment can be difficult. Often there is a lot of spiritual sweat involved because we're not ready to see what in fact, the soul is clearly showing us we need to do. We create aversions and distractions and we flail around as if we're drowning, or we pretend that we're lost.[29]'

We must be willing to take the action that we are guided to take by our intuitive intelligence. Raising our vibration and using discernment are two things that must be done together. Otherwise, what we do with this idea of energetic protection is abuse ourselves. We might say to ourselves,

*I can continue to stay in this abusive relationship because I can always hold a higher vibration than the external evidence. I can continue to let that friend be mean to me and take advantage of me because I can hold a higher vibration than they can, and therefore I'm protected.*

That is against our divine nature.

We are acting in bad faith because our intuition is tapping us on the shoulder, saying,

*We're done here. We don't need to be here, and I love you, and this is over now.*

But because of a lack of spiritual self-esteem, which is the courage to follow our God nature, we find ourselves in unnecessary suffering. If we are not taking the action that our intuition calls us to take and creating a life that corresponds with what we are saying we want and desire, we offer ourselves no protection. We leave ourselves wide open because we're betraying ourselves by being incongruent, and there's no protection in that. We must come into congruence with what it is that we're saying. Congruence is,

---

29 Meggan Watterson, *Reveal*, 2013

*I'm a match between my faith and my actions in the world.*

If our actions are fearful, fuelled by separation thinking, we are not the representative of that highest vibration. Then we'll see a scary, scary world. We will say,

*But Ricci-Jane, I had this thought-form attach itself to me!*

Or,

*That person put an evil eye on me!*

Or,

*I forgot to whitelight my car, and I had an accident!*

I will nod and agree.

*Yes, you were curating or corresponding to that as truth. You were allowing that story, that belief, to collapse the wave function and make it real for you.*

If we want to see it, we'll find it. So, where do we want to leap? What frequency do we want to embody? What version of reality do we want to live at when every version exists? With what are we choosing to correspond? For me, it's simple — the highest possible vibration that I can hold every day (which will be different every day). But as a permanent shift from fear to love takes place in my subconscious/subtle body through my devotion, it will be consistently high. That's the task of my life as my highest form of service. That's how I protect myself. Better yet, that's how I circle all consciousness in my embrace. That is my task.

In a workshop in which I was sharing this subject with some of my students training to become teachers of Intuitive Intelligence, one of the students asked me how we avoid getting tired holding our vibration high all the time.

I remember laughing. I replied,

*It's not like lifting weights!*

But in truth, this fear is common. It is born of our belief that we are doing this work of increasing our vibration all by ourselves. In reality, we dissolve the boundaries between ourselves and the Superconscious Mind. The more we overcome our belief in separation through our actions, the more we open to our unlimited capacity as pure vibration. No effort is required when we are operating from this perspective. There's no effort in holding a high vibration if we correspond with what we indeed are. Initially, it does take spiritual sweat. It takes discipline, and it takes a commitment to show up and to live in congruence with our faith. Ultimately, it becomes our state of being.

Another student asked in the same teaching workshop,

*So my crystals are useless now? Shall I throw them out?*

To this, I said, no. I love crystals. I love to have these beautiful objects in my home just as I love books, and I love plants, and I love artwork. If it brings us joy, it's supporting us, holding a higher vibration. Anything that makes us feel good and does not cause harm to others is not a problem. It's about moving away from that idea that,

*I must have this in order to be energetically safe.*

## Empowerment versus dependence

The responsibility of this new perspective on energetic protection is not a comfortable one. It isn't an easy path. It's much easier just to be someone who indulges our clients' fears or our friends or our family or even our own fears. It's a choice now to recognise how extraordinary we are. We live in an extraordinary age. We know that the world is accelerating. The length of time of a second is no longer what it once was.

Literally, time is speeding up. We live in accelerated political climates where the changes that we're seeing in our governments are happening at such a rapid rate and with such chaos. The systems of power are falling, and the economic world order is collapsing. The environmental crisis is constantly changing at a rate that we can't even begin to fathom. We're even increasing our electromagnetic rate, and so is the planet. We know from readings of the Earth's field (often referred to as the Earth's heartbeat) — Schumann Resonance — that there have been multiple enormous leaps forward in accelerated resonance. In every way, we live in an extraordinary, accelerated age beyond the end times.

What we're being asked to do on the path of service is even greater than it once was. We're invited now to surrender fear in every way. We're asked to meet our power and to offer that to others. To be a match for this extraordinary time, sometimes we're going to have to disappoint people who are not yet there. Sometimes we are not going to be able to comfort their suffering. We're going to have to say,

*What if that's not true? What if that suffering is not real? The reality is, if you believe in a world that you need protection from, you will live in a world from which you need protection.*

How do we serve in that paradigm? If we are vulnerable and afraid, it may feel like the best thing is to comfort them in that and accommodate that, and send them off to someone who can tell them that the 'bad guy' is gone. Or we can help them meet their power. Even if we feel they're not ready for it. If we are being shown someone living in fear, serving them spiritually is not to perpetuate their belief in the conditions of fear. It is to help them understand whether they are ready consciously or not.

We all need the conditions where we're scaffolded and supported to meet our own fear. I don't indulge my students, and many of them don't like that at first, and then they do like it because they see that their power is their own. Some people walk away from me, though, because they need to go and be with someone who will heal them or fix them or tell them what the problems are and take away the bad guys for them. I simply want to say to them,

*What if you just choose not to live in that world anymore?*

If we live in a world where something is *other* to us, something is outside of us, and we believe that we need protection from that thing, we will keep having experiences that will call forward the people, places, events and entities that confirm that belief. If we do not choose to live in that world anymore, we will no longer live in that world. We know by now that we can't just make up our Conscious Reasoning Mind. We need to go into our subconscious basement and allow that fear to be met face on. I cannot emphasise this enough. And it is the difference between those of us who will lead the new paradigm and those who will sit in our trinkets and superstitions and continue to perpetuate the misery and suffering of others in the name of spirituality. Some want to continue to sit in their fear and pretend it's spirituality.

If we believe that there are non-physical entities, for example, that are outside of us that we are somehow vulnerable to, we must get real about where those things come from. They come from within. They come from within us because we are the entire universe in a microcosm. We are projecting our consciousness out and living in it. This isn't something that I'm sharing because I want to say there are not people out there who are having an awful time and feel like their boundaries are vulnerable and that bad things are trying to get them. I'm sharing this because millions of people feel that way, and we can do something about that. We can emancipate people from their fear. We can wake them to their spiritual fierceness rather than perpetuating the conditions in which people believe that fear exists. Fear does not exist, not in truth, not beyond the illusion, not beyond the collection of false beliefs that keep us in a prison, not beyond our need for it to exist. Our need for it to exist is to direct us back to truth. Love is all there is.

We simply have to be willing.

*Am I willing to attune to the frequency of God to the infinite to the unlimited? And if so, how many times? How many times a day am I willing to do that?*

It will become so second nature to us that with every breath, we bring ourselves into the vibration that we want to be living in no matter what news we get or how disapproving people are of us. We simply do not live in that world because everything we need is provided by the universe within.

# Chapter 10

# Rebellious Acceptance and Radical Advantageousness

*"For those of you born in the [West], you have an obligation to be a rebel. It is not a choice. It is an obligation. You have an obligation to be a rebel/revolutionary to some extent. Every spiritual avatar is a rebel. You don't think Jesus was a rebel, or Mohammed? Everyone worth their salt is a rebel. Freedom requires rebellious action. The conscious use of what is worthy of being challenged in a society. You have an obligation".*

—Caroline Myss

The infinite doesn't simply correspond to our belief about it. It does it with direct intent. As *A Course in Miracles* states, 'You see what you expect, and you expect what you have invited. Your perception is the result of your invitation coming to you as you sent for it. Whose manifestations would you see? Of whose presence would you be convinced? For you will believe in what you manifest? And, as you look out, so will you see in.'[30] Can I believe that the infinite is all-powerful and that it is my partner and still sit in feelings of low self-worth? No, I am breaking the law. The universe will behave in accordance with my beliefs.

If we hold feelings of low self-worth, life will seem like a living hell, and God will appear to be punishing or testing us at every turn. As we know, this is simply not possible in truth, but we have to look to ourselves. How can we heal the belief in separation, the dualism that makes us think that God's power is separate from us and heaven is a place we can only access when we die? Intuitive intelligence is remembering that we are a divine piece of a benevolent God that is always working on our behalf. We have to keep walking this path of breaking the habit of unworthiness, of breaking the habit of negative self-talk, of breaking the habit of believing that we are victims of our circumstances. This is what it is to be spiritually radical. To be a spiritual rebel is to reject the programming that keeps us concretised to our human identity at the expense of our divinity.

## Rebellious acceptance

When we talk about making this permanent shift from fear to love, a perfect place to start is with the notion of rebellious acceptance. Rebellious acceptance is the idea that we are not arguing with reality anymore so that when life events happen, we don't say,

*Things should not be this way; I should not be punished like this; it isn't fair that that person has cancer, it's not right that children are harmed.*

---

30 *A Course in Miracles* | T-12.VII.5:1-5 Accessed at: https://acim.org/acim/en/s/161#5:1-5

When we think or speak like this, we argue with what is. Rebellious acceptance is when we lay down our arms; we move out of the experience of life as constantly combative, or that life is trying to harm us or take something from us, or that things have gone wrong, or God has forgotten us. Why is this rebellious? Because everything in the world has taught us that we have a right to withhold acceptance, that we must fight for our survival, that life is a battleground. Rebellious acceptance is fuelled by the desire to resist that dominant convention and to choose differently for ourselves. We no longer fulfil the status quo of believing that *life's a bitch and then you die.* The indoctrination to the idea that life is a struggle. We won't be controlled in that way anymore.

Rebellious acceptance is non-judgment. Events are not good or bad. They just are. This perception stops the war with ourselves and the world. This prevents that state of being in which all of the stress hormones are constantly active, where we're constantly in our sympathetic nervous system. We're in a state of feeling under threat. Instead, we begin to receive the world through benevolence. We say,

*I don't know why this is happening, but I am curious to find out, and I'm not going to argue with it. I'm not going to argue and say things should be different because in doing that, I take myself into emotional chaos.*

If we are in a state of constant emotional chaos, then we are placing our attention on chaos. We're inviting more of that chaos. In the beginning, we may say,

*Well, this is because someone else did this to me. I didn't invite this chaos. I didn't want that person to do this thing to me or for me to find out I owed $10,000 in tax or whatever it is that triggers you into a state of chaos.*

When we change our minds about the events in our lives, when we can sit outside of judgement of good or bad, we begin to change the chaos response inside our bodies. We begin to trigger new neural pathways, up-regulating or down-regulating different genes and altering the chemicals producing the hormone response in the body. We start to see a benevolent world. We begin to be curious about the events of our life rather than assuming that everything means something has gone wrong.

To come into harmony, the first step is to come on board or to get on board with reality as it is. It bears repeating that this is not approving of circumstances. We're not saying we should approve of people mistreating us or having to spend money we don't have, or the state of the world and the state of the way that children are treated around the globe. It isn't approving. It's simply withdrawing all of that wasted energy from arguing with what is. The only place of change, the only thing that will change the current status quo, is to lay down our arms and to stop fighting. Because that fighting, that war, that chaos, is calling more and more and more of that to us.

When we go out into the world with anger and rage at the world's injustice, we create the conditions that demand more rage and injustice. All minds are joined. It cannot be any other way. What is the next step? How do we go beyond rebellious acceptance? Because, of course, that is only a step. It's a mighty step, and it is a requirement that that step happens because it's what opens our hearts.

## Forgiveness

To be spiritually radical in this way, we have to find ways to forgive ourselves. We have to go into forgiveness of the circumstances of our life because guilt and shame caused by unforgiveness are the most toxic human emotions of them all. Acceptance of what is is the first step in making change. The next step after rebellious acceptance is forgiveness. Without forgiveness, we are not on board with events as they currently are. It is not enough to say,

*I forgive, but I will never forget.*

That is the ego saying,

*I actually don't forgive. I will think hateful thoughts about you every day, but I'll sound like I'm nobler and better than you by saying I'm sorry or I forgive you for your actions against me.*

It's not forgiveness if we keep a vendetta going or withhold our love from that person. Now that might be quite challenging, especially if we believe from our human sight that we have had something terrible done to us by another. It requires great courage to surrender the human perspective, but we must because it cannot free us. The human perspective is a dream state. It is an illusory state where we believe we are separate, finite, and vulnerable. When we start thinking like God, we say,

*Even though I do not understand why these events needed to occur, I am willing to believe that everything is working on my behalf.*

From that perspective, we begin to forgive the events of our lives, and that forgiveness is the medicine that allows our hearts to go from bitter to better. We see with symbolic sight the meaning rather than focussing on the cause.

Recently, my family experienced emotional bullying from an external influence. We are a blended family, and someone on my partner's side engaged in behaviour that caused extreme stress on our family unit. I kept going into my devotional practices seeing a peaceful outcome and holding the highest possible resolution for all, especially our children. But nothing changed, and the behaviour intensified over months to become intolerable for us all to manage. My wise mama called me one day, and I unloaded my stress onto her. She guided me to see that I wasn't in rebellious acceptance. I was holding forgiveness in a performative way. I would often get up from my devotion and start imaginary conversations with this person as I tried to wrestle some control over the situation. I turned up to my devotion with an agenda — I wanted this problem gone from my life. I was focused on the cause. This person was messing with my peace. I wanted God to 'fix' them. I didn't have my spiritual goggles on, even though I was pretending to myself that I did. With my mother's guidance, I acknowledged my agenda and got on board with true forgiveness, which is the acceptance of what is. This is what is right now. This has to be serving me. Then, instead, I could ask,

*What's in this for me? What's the deeper meaning of this for me?*

Within 24 hours, the way that this situation was serving me landed, and I set in motion a series of life-changing actions, which I simply had not been able to see before because I thought I knew the solution. I believed that this person changing their behaviour was what I needed. It turned out that was far from the truth. This person was serving my awakening, taking me closer to a truth I had been resisting. From there, I could let this person off the hook. I could let myself off the hook, and I could see clearly for the first time without my ideas of how things should be. I could forgive this person and this situation.

Forgiveness is rebellious acceptance of what is. Nothing has gone wrong, and I don't want to waste the opportunity to extract wisdom from these events by being bitter and constantly saying they should not have happened. If there is a higher meaning or higher purpose to those events, I want to unlock them so that I can continue my soul's awakening. This is a masterful perspective. We are here to see that the events of our lives, one of many lifetimes, have never gone wrong. God has never forgotten us, and if we go back to the laws, we understand that we crafted this existence. I curated it according to my belief, and now I'm ready to believe something far better, and I know that the first step is this forgiveness or rebellious acceptance.

Some vital aspects of this must be stated clearly here. These events are not created from our Reasoning Conscious Mind, and they were not made at only the individual level of consciousness either. In no way am I suggesting we individually manifested our abuser because our thoughts were wonky or we are experiencing racial injustice because we didn't hold our consciousness at the right level. We are never acting in isolation. The imbalances in the world are part of the collective unconscious. But we must take personal responsibility, especially those of us who are not in survival mode because of our life circumstances, to correct the error in the collective consciousness. We do this by looking at our subconscious programs.

In addition, we must understand that the adoption of this attitude is not about attempting to prevent life from happening to us. Instead, we change our perception of the things that occur and in so doing, neutralise the emotional charge in the body and open to the possibility of the miracle concealed within.

## Radical advantageousness

Radical advantageousness is when our lives are in service to creating an advantage or favourability to ourselves, those around us and the collective good at large. It is not enough to simply sit in neutrality. It isn't enough to withdraw our attention from the things that we do not want. It is far more powerful to move into a positive receipt of those things. By that, I mean that we can see that everything is working to our advantage.

Rebellious acceptance leads to forgiveness, which leads to radical advantageousness. It is not enough to just not be negative. It is not enough just to withhold negative judgments of others. We need to commit to living in accordance with these laws with our whole being, to change the ecology of the environment that we exist in, and everywhere we go by holding a state of radical advantageousness.

*How can my life be of benefit to the collective?*

Think of it like this. We walk into a group, whether it's a group that we're teaching or a group that we work with or our own family, and we discern where their vibration is. We feel into how they're all doing, and we notice whatever we notice. Wherever they are, we make it our personal commitment to bring a state of being that is higher than that, and that because of our commitment to knowing that all minds are joined, we can transform wherever they are, no matter how good or bad, into a higher state. We bring a favourability to the situation. We are the unknown advantage. We all know someone like that, who walks into the room and lights it up, whose presence seems to make tasks easier, or seemingly brings luck wherever they go.

In radical advantageousness, we're not simply thinking,

*What can I get out of my life for me?*

Instead, we are motivated by,

*How may I serve?*

If you've been wondering what your life purpose is, please put that concern down now, your purpose is the same as all others. It is service. We are here to serve the awakening of consciousness in all. We do not do this for ourselves alone. When we move into radical advantageousness, we're getting over ourselves. We're no longer thinking,

*Well, I've got a good reason to be in a bad mood today, and I'm allowed to stay in that mood and pass it on to everybody else.*

We think that when things happen to us that are not in accordance with what we think should occur, we are entitled to then bring everybody else around us down to our level, and that's what we do all the time.

As we know by now, we are more powerful than we realise, and we entrain other people to whatever vibration we're holding. This is a massive paradigm shift. We don't even think about doing that. We just do it. We don't think,

*Oh, if I take this terrible mood into this group or this environment or to my family, then I might be causing harm to them.*

We think we're justified. We genuinely don't question that. We believe that suffering entitles us to share that suffering around. But if we go back to rebellious acceptance, we see that

God consciousness is always benevolently working on our behalf and we surrender and forgive that event.

Then we can move into radical advantageousness where we can be the cause of happiness for others. We take our environment, whatever it is, to a higher level.

*I prepare everything with my radical advantageousness, and it isn't false positivity because I've done the work. I have cleared my unforgiveness, I have moved the bitterness out of my heart, and it's effortless then to attune to a higher frequency.*

We so quickly entrain to the fear frequencies because we do not know we have another choice. It is indoctrinated into our collective unconscious that fear is the normal state of being. We're suspicious of people if they seem to be happy or not affected by the events of their life in the way that we are.

That's why we tell our stories of suffering so frequently because we want to get an audience for them. We want to keep getting confirmation that we're okay to keep our bitterness. The reason that we do that is we genuinely understand that it's not okay to indulge our fixations, but if someone says to us,

*Oh my God, I'm so sorry, that should never have happened to you.*

And we get constant sympathy. We're at least dumbing down or drowning out that voice that says,

*No, you don't need to stay here. You're entitled to be free.*

We're so afraid of that power. What if that is true? What if I cannot remain in bitterness and unforgiveness towards those who did things or life events or the state of the world? Part of us will want to play God in the world. We want to be the judge and jury. We want to spread our form of justice. We think we know what is best. But we're still learning how to think like God right now. We're not there yet. As God, we're not looking at one event in one lifetime to sentence it as right or wrong. We're looking at the whole unfolding of the soul's awakening from the beginning of time until the end. It takes outstanding commitment to practice perceiving in this way, but we are all on that path already, so why not just go to the next level?

I heard Marianne Williamson share this insight from *A Course in Miracles*. When we stay in bitterness and unforgiveness, we prevent the download of the most blessed version of our life. We prevent the miracle from manifesting. But it is not lost. It is held in trust for us by God. The miracle, the highest version of our life, the correction of perception, cannot download into our bitterness, our judgements, and unforgiveness. The other thing to know about this is every time we forgive what's right in front of us, even though it looks insurmountable, we are accelerating our awakening.[31] But more importantly, God goes into bat for us, goes into our subconscious and rewires the program. Even though that's invisible to our consciousness, every time we make a choice for love over fear, we get support.

What will it take for us to start thinking like God? What will it take for us to surrender our limited human perspective and begin, even if we cannot see the bigger picture yet, to trust that things have not gone wrong? It's a truly blessed and joyful state of being to live in. It isn't about letting other people's actions go unpunished. It's simply knowing that we are not the one who needs to set the scales right. It is not our job. This is where discernment comes in. To forgive the other does not mean that we then need to spend any time with them, as we learned in the previous chapter. There doesn't have to be any exchange in human reality at all. It's vital for us to know this

---

31 Accessed at: https://www.youtube.com/watch?v=a4tl_AAxQao

because what happens when we truly forgive is our heart is wide open, and then suddenly we want to reconnect with that person. But at their level of awakening and consciousness, they are genuinely not a person that we should be spending time with. Discerning where we place ourselves and who we spend time with is vital to spiritual maturity.

Forgiving is not the same as condoning, and we need to know that there may be things that we need to do to take action in local reality. We might need to report that person's activities to the police, or we might need to take steps that mean that an event can never happen again. That might mean leaving the marriage, or it might mean not spending time with a friend, whatever it is for us. But that is done as an act of self-love, not an attempt to punish the other person for their actions because it is not our job to bring the scales of justice into balance. Let God take care of that. In so doing, we allow the miracle to download from superconsciousness to allow our life to come into its highest and most graceful form.

# Chapter 11

# Superconscious Gloriousness

*"If you are not shining, you are darkness."*
*—Adyashanti*

Superconscious gloriousness is our natural state. It is us without fear and doubt. Up to now, we have experienced only fleeting glimpses of our gloriousness. The only thing to do is remove the impediments to knowing what we are. Gloriousness comes when we know that everything in our lives is always working on our behalf. We live in a state of deep trust and certainty in ourselves. We feel the benevolence of God guiding us, even when we may not completely understand how or why. Gloriousness comes from the faith that something more profound, higher, and vaster guides our lives. Gloriousness is a state of profound awakening to that which we are. It is typified by profound self-worth, resplendence, joy, lightness of being, laughter, kindness, compassion, generosity and reverence. When we meet someone who embodies her gloriousness, it is unmissable. There is the presence of a light that appears to emerge from within. I recall being on retreat at a Buddhist monastery on the Sunshine Coast in Queensland. I was a volunteer in residence. There was a young monk there whose very presence was radiant. One evening our group of volunteers joined to listen to him teach. He shared deep wisdom but what I recall most profoundly was his joy. He was quick to laugh and easeful in his presence. He was glorious.

Superconscious gloriousness is the state beyond fear. It is not the absence of fear. Fear will rise as long as we are in our bodies on this Earth. But the choice to live beyond fear is the state of gloriousness, in which we choose to meet fear with curiosity and light-heartedness as we have learned. We do not fear *fear* because we know our Godliness.

## Guiltlessness is a pre-condition of gloriousness

Guiltlessness is the highest form of forgiveness. We recognise that there is nothing to forgive in the first place. This can only be our reality when we have complete faith in the superconsciousness guiding us all the time. We no longer judge ourselves or others, and that lack of judgement permits our hearts to remain open. This is vital because of the ultimate truth. We are one with God. And we are all One. If I hold my heart closed to another, I keep my heart closed to myself, and I hold myself apart from God. Gloriousness cannot exist here. Above all else, gloriousness requires that we overcome our belief in separation. We cannot see glory in ourselves if we cannot see it in another and vice versa. We cannot see God in ourselves if we cannot see it in another. For gloriousness is our Superconscious nature shining through.

# What prevents our gloriousness?

Lack of conviction is the greatest malaise that prevents our access to our true gloriousness. We are lazy. We jump from one thought to the next, one idea to another, without the devotion required to birth a new state of being into reality. We claim we want to meet our truth, power, grace, love, glory, and superconscious self, and then we dilly dally. Our attention drifts away. We get distracted by the next shiny thing we see. Luckily, our Superconscious nature constantly corrects us back to the task at hand, the very and only purpose for our lives, but like untrained puppies, we stray off the path so quickly. *A Course in Miracles* reminds us that miracles derive from conviction[32]. When *Spiritually Fierce* came out, a reader asked me what else she could read to attain more knowledge on this subject. I entirely support deep study, but I was slightly taken aback by her request. She had just that moment finished the book, which is full of devotional practices to support the integration of the knowledge so that it turns to wisdom. I asked her how long she had spent with each practice. Not surprisingly, she had read through them but not gone into practising them. I asked her to consider making herself a student of the text for some time before moving on.

If we all chose to sit at the feet of one sacred text for the rest of our lives, we would benefit profoundly. In the age of unlimited access to information, our self-discipline determines how deeply we go into any idea, philosophy or practice. Consumption of knowledge is as much of an addiction as any other. We gorge ourselves on the new instead of reigning our

---

32 *A Course in Miracles*, T-1.I.14:1-3 Accessed at: https://acim.org/acim/en/s/53#14:1-3

focus in and surrendering to genuine transformation. This takes time and leads to the next thing that delays our gloriousness.

We think surrendering to our Superconscious gloriousness is one and done (to borrow a phrase from Elisha Halpin). Our surrender is more akin to the process of decomposition. This word emerged during a circle I was facilitating recently. We were working with the energy of the dark goddess, as her archetypal energy invited us to break down yet another layer of illusion. Just when we think there's no more to surrender, there is, of course, always more. The deep work of deep faith is the work of surrender of all illusion. All life is a glorious and terrible consciousness experiment. Decomposing samsaric longing, letting the layers of egoic identity release all the stuff we've been clinging to, allowing us to become fertile ground for love and truth. But we cannot rush this phase, the phase of decomposing, of tearing down old structures. We must welcome the darkness of the void before we rush to create the new.

*I am not that. I am not this. I am unbecoming. I am dissolving. I am nothing before I become everything.*

This is a noble and humble phase of awakening that will visit us many times in our lives if we're doing the deep work. Sometimes we are creating, and sometimes we are destroying. And it's all divine. We do not take everything personally. We come to recognise *it is not about us.*

All this effort and spiritual sweat is not to awaken to more of the self, but to get over the self. The juiciest paradox of all is that we must become nothing to become everything. We often turn up to our spiritual path, seeking to become 'something'. Or to get something. Or to fix something. We are motivated by the desire to improve ourselves, make more of ourselves, to awaken ourselves. Very quickly, we come to understand that it isn't about us at all if we are doing the deep work of a deep faith.

On the same retreat where a student accused me of manipulating her feelings, I came face to face with the archetypal energy Hindu goddess, Kali Ma. For days after the incident with the student, I held a sense of injustice in response to her words and actions. I didn't speak this out loud. I didn't seek to communicate with her. I held the indignation in my body, even as I was sweating on the yoga mat and practising hours of meditation. My ego was in overdrive, and I was lost to the present experience. I wanted justice. Well, justice was delivered, but not how my ego wanted it. One night as we completed a circle in our open-air shala, with the nighttime sounds of the jungle all around, bodies warm from the humid air, I felt her. Kali Ma symbolises rebirth through destruction. She is the life that emerges from death. She is the Divine Mother and the Dark Mother, and when she approaches, we bow humbly. She does not come lightly, and I secretly hoped I was intuiting her presence on behalf of another. But I knew it wasn't so.

I sensed her standing at the edge of the shala, gaze fixed on me. She encircled me in a ring of fire. I felt my body getting even warmer. I didn't resist. I was honoured by her presence.

*Yes, I need this. I know how egoic my thoughts have been. This is good. Surrender.*

When the process felt complete, I got up from my mat and made my way to bed, impressed with myself for so readily accepting the Dark Goddess and confident my mind was now set to right. I can laugh now at my foolishness. Instead, in the coming days, in the hot, sticky climate of Bali, I was covered from head to toe in an increasingly itchy, red rash. The fire had left its mark. I received the treatment I needed, but the rash was slow to depart. I understood the meaning. I wanted to wrap this event up with a neat bow and move on. But Kali Ma is not interested in superficial transformation. The remainder of my time on retreat was humbling. Kali Ma truly held me in the fire. Through judgement, I had placed walls between the student and myself. I had engaged in dualism. I wanted justice, not the deeper meaning of how this was serving me. I had to get over myself. This was what the retreat space offered me, even though I had a different agenda.

It is in surrendering the idea of us as an individual identity we truly begin to awaken. We must get over ourselves, our ego identity, to become empty. Humility is being devoid of the longing for anything for ourselves. We then become everything. We recognise that our spiritual awakening is in service to our all-ness, not our ego identity. We want to liberate all because we realise that is what we are. I am that. To surrender the ego identity to become God-identified. This is when we make the all-important step from *getting to giving*.

## The Stages of Glory Awakening

### 1. From getting to giving

When we are afraid, we have forgotten we are God. When we are in this state of forgetting, we are in survival mode, looking only to our welfare. We assess each situation with our human senses, and we ask, what can I get out of this situation? How will it benefit me? It matters not if the benefit is to the detriment of the other. We have forgotten that we are One, so it does not matter if our survival means harm to others. In this state, we are constantly in a mentality of lack. We believe that there is not enough for everyone, and so if they have, then I have not. Jealousy, self-doubt and shame plague us in this survival state.

Why shame? Shame is the ego's modus operandi at this level of our awakening. Because we are acting against our true nature, and we know it subconsciously even if we will not admit it to ourselves, then we are in a constant state of guilt-induced shame. As such, we see everyone and everything around us through this lens of guilt. We project our feelings of shame and justify taking and getting through this projection.

Luckily for us, our true nature is more significant than our fear, and our soul's yearning will eventually activate in all of us. We begin by waking up to the feeling that there is a deeper meaning to our lives. We notice a generosity emerging in us. We want to give. At first, we may not even know what we want to give, but we want it so strongly that sometimes we turn our lives upside down on this hunch. This is when we might go into business for ourselves, be overcome by the desire to write a book or take up a new study path. We want to give to the world. We want to make a difference. Our gloriousness is agitating us awake. When the divine invitation arrived in me to start the Institute, I was a woman on fire. Nothing else I did satisfied me in the way that my service did. I wanted to be with the creative heat moving through me at all times. I had energy for days. I was nourished by something so much greater than my physical form.

At that point, I had ignored the yearning of my soul for several years. I was in denial of what God wanted for me. It was a torturous existence. When I finally surrendered, it was as if the floodgates opened, and I was swept along with all the truth that I had been denying. I want to add here that it does not mean that beginning the Institute was effortless. It was not. In the first year, I had very few clients in the first year and made some significant errors. But the energy available to me was superhuman because I was so motivated by this ache to serve! There was no doubt in my mind, and any challenges I met were never insurmountable. I felt as though I had God on my team, for indeed I did. I was flowing with my life rather than resisting the call to sacred service. I was in bliss.

## 2. From giving to receiving

Now we are on the path that leads us back to our truth, and there is no going back, thankfully. Sure, we might resist, but we have handed over the reins to something greater than our human identity. We have handed our lives to God, which is to say to ourselves in all our glory. Now we notice that it is not enough for us to give. What we could give from the human dimension is simply not enough. That more remarkable part of ourselves is still agitating us awake, and we listen to it with more devotion. Our dedication, our inner discipline means that it is temporary when we stray back into fear. We are quick to notice our error, and we correct ourselves. We are listening now. And in that listening, we have shifted from *giving to receiving.* We are aware that anything worthy of giving is not coming from our human self but our God-self, and to provide that, we must be willing to let it fill us. We must receive our gloriousness into us without hesitation, for that is what we are yearning to share. Now we have met our glory face to face, we desire all to know this truth, for it is a shared truth. Now, our only desire is to be the divine channel for grace. Anything we do in our human reality is only a vehicle for that divine expression. Now we are simply being what we are.

I was conducting an energetic evaluation on a student recently. In this session, we identify the dominant negative self-belief stored in the subconscious. My student is a professionally successful woman and highly motivated to be a cause for good in the world. But in her subconscious was anger that she would not fulfil her purpose in this life. This confused her as she believed she lived a purposeful, service-driven life. What was clear to me was that, whilst this was true, she was hiding from her God nature. Undoubtedly, she is a sacred leader, but this part of herself she has kept in the closet. Her subconscious was carrying the emotional collateral of this, which of course, meant her vibrational frequency was off. She was being invited to be all in with her sacred truth, for this was the bigger picture of her life, and until she overcame the fear of judgement from others, she would not set herself free to be all that she is.

## 3. Beingness

Beingness is the final phase of remembering our gloriousness. We just let ourselves be. There is so much peace in this statement that it may not even be possible for us to imagine such a state from where we currently stand. But we must not give up. We must keep taking the steps towards our being. Without a doubt, these following practices are the most accelerated path I know to that state of being our gloriousness.

We unbelieve ourselves. We must never be afraid of giving up belief and all our ideas of ourselves. Who we are exists beyond belief. The less we believe about ourselves, the closer we are to our God nature. Definitions are dead weights that prevent us from awakening to the truth. We are God-consciousness, pure and unlimited. Any other category, definition, diagnosis, quiz, map, chart is fixing us to time and space. We are then further anchored into a false, temporary reality that gives the ego satisfaction and even relief from the personal responsibility of coming home to the truth that we are God. Read that again. Despite our yearning to come home, we're desperately yearning to be relieved from that responsibility. Don't fall for it. Become nothing. It's the only way to meet ourselves as what we are.

The process of getting to know ourselves on this path of awakening is vital. But if we stop there, we have wasted our efforts. As I've stated before, self-awareness is not the same as self-realisation. Ultimately, *know thyself* means we meet ourselves as God. If we think it means identifying ourselves as a sun sign Scorpio, moon sign Pisces, manifestor-generator, INFJ, Pleiadian descendant, starseed, indigo child, or any of the myriad ways we box ourselves in and justify our behaviour, then we've missed the point. We've created more division and more dualism. If this is a step on the path to unknowing ourselves, then, by all means, embrace the process. But don't stop at the labels. There is only one name we carry, and that is God.

## How to get to our gloriousness

### 1.  *Meet shame with joy*

Shame and guilt are the enemies of our gloriousness. When we follow this path back to our superconscious intuition, we will continually meet the limits of our comfort zone of feeling safe to be glorious. Like explorers who keep stepping into new terrain, we will feel lost each time we step into another level of our gloriousness. Because we are not comfortable with the mystery, with inhabiting the void, we will doubt ourselves. This doubt allows fear to run rampant. To meet our own glory feels joyous. And joy is death to the ego. The ego, that part of us that believes it is separate from God, will go to its number one weapon of self-destruction — shame (and its bedfellow, guilt).

We have all experienced this before. For whatever reason, we are feeling joyful. Perhaps we are given a beautiful gift or have a good thing happen to us. For a brief and beautiful moment, our glory is set free, and it begins to dance wildly about us. And then, without warning, shame or guilt hit us hard. Who are we to feel good about this gift or event when someone else is going without? Or who are we to think we are worthy of such a lucky break? We've done things that make us unworthy. We are guilty. It's important to note here that all these thoughts are happening at the subconscious level of our minds. That means more than likely, the emotion of shame and guilt hits us without even having a conscious thought. This is so much more dangerous because we can't rationalise it. It consumes us bodily, and we then look for evidence to support the truth of the emotions. We find a story of pain to justify the emotion, and so it sticks because now we have proof. In an instant, we have abandoned our joyful feeling. We didn't fight for our good feelings. Yet we ran towards the negative emotion. Why is that?

It's because we are trained all our lives to privilege fear. Joy is strange. It is less familiar to us. We are creatures of habit, and our pattern has been to attend to our fear. We need an antidote. We need something greater than our fear. We need to practice a greater state of being than we currently are. And this is how to do it.

When a feeling of joy alights upon us, we must make a conscious choice to expand that feeling state in disproportion to the event that caused the joy feeling. In other words, we are creating a state of being that is greater than our current environment. It is easier to leap upwards when we are already occupying a higher state of being, so use the existing feeling to leap higher.

**Here's the practice:**

Close down your eyes, if you are safe to do so, and breathe into the centre of your chest. The anatomical and metaphysical heart combine to create the most powerful centre of your electromagnetic body. In other words, the feeling state you generate moves out into the cosmos far more powerfully from here than from any other place of your being.

With your eyes closed and your breath fully conscious, you are withdrawing your senses from the superficial world and moving into your superconsciousness. Here it is easy to expand into joyous feelings. Feel, sense, think or imagine the feeling state expanding like a ball of light, increasing with every breath. Feel, sense, think or imagine it expands as far as your imagination will take it, perhaps even consuming the whole world in your joy.

Do this as often as you experience a joyful feeling state, for in doing so, you are breaking the habit of being human, and you are inviting your gloriousness to become your default setting.

*2. Sweat for God*

The choice to inhabit our natural state of gloriousness is not something that is magically bestowed upon us. Consistent, daily, moment by moment commitment is what will turn our longing into reality. There is no magic bullet to this state of spiritual maturity. It is an inside job, and nothing outside of us can take us there. This self-reliance is the willingness to hand our lives over to our superconsciousness and invite that part of us to run the show. This will also require a commitment to developing our inner soul fire, our resilience. What does this mean exactly? Instead of surrendering to every troubling thought or losing all motivation with every bad day we have, we must cultivate an inner resilience that allows us to navigate the highs and lows of human reality. We must not abandon ourselves in a heartbeat to whatever external event or negative self-belief crosses our minds. What would it take to maintain a still point at the centre of the storm? Life situations will happen. Our commitment to moving to the impersonal view of life events is a profound step to occupying our glory.

**Here's the practice:**

Each morning before you rise, join your mind to the mind of God. Invite your glory to be the lens through which you perceive the world. As such, bless everyone and everything you meet that day before you even rise. Pray only for blessings to rain down upon all. Beginning your day this way is a great step towards developing inner resilience and consistency that typifies an awakened being.

*3.    Keep your consciousness pure*

Above all else, we should discern where we place our precious consciousness. The conversations we have, the books we read, the movies we watch, the social media we absorb, all these things are programming our consciousness. We need to ask ourselves only this,

*Is this in accordance with my gloriousness? Does this allow me to see as God sees?*

If the answer is no, it is in our best interest to end the conversation, turn off the movie, choose another text, or close down the browser. The fastest way to attune to our gloriousness is to focus upon those things that reflect our truth to us. Read sacred texts, meditate upon images of enlightened beings, listen to music that reminds us of our soul nature.

We do not awaken to our gloriousness for our gain. We do it because not to do it is to deny God. To deny God is to deny the truth that we are One. When we awaken, we awaken for all. To hide our gloriousness is to conceal that truth within all of all. We cannot ask others to do what we will not do for ourselves. *A Course in Miracles* tells us that teaching is demonstrating. We must be the living, breathing example of God's glory on behalf of all. It is a sacred privilege and divine responsibility for those of us for whom this is possible.

And so it is.

# Conclusion

# Meeting Ourselves as Superconscious Leaders

*"We work at building you with trembling hands*
*Piling one atom upon the other.*
*But who can ever finish you,*
*You great cathedral [?]"*

—*Rainer Maria Rilke*

I trust God. I had these words inked on the inside of my right forearm whilst on retreat in Bali in November 2019. It was just before the world shut down due to the Covid-19 Pandemic. I didn't know that then, of course. I didn't realise that it would be the last retreat I could lead for a very long time. I also didn't know that these words would change everything. My marriage was over within months. My entire life, unrecognisable. A wise friend asked me what I expected when making such a powerful declaration, permanently inked on my body? Tattooing this statement on my body was a bold declaration that I was prepared to be congruent with my faith. At that time, I was not yet there.

These words represent my soul contract in this life, and of course, that means they are my service. My purpose is to teach others to know that they are God. When I say *I trust God*, as we have explored throughout this book, I really mean *I trust myself.* I teach others to trust themselves.

I trust God is my soul contract. Not surprisingly, the opposite statement is my dominant fear.

*I don't trust God.*

It's that sacred wound that I have been wrestling with the last few years. After I left my husband, that God-guided action, I spent two years in the wilderness of my being. If I had thought because it was God-inspired that my exit from one phase of my soul's awakening to the next would be simple, I was wrong. It was the beginning of a necessary descent to the underworld of my being to be stripped of illusion and doubt. It was time to meet my dominant fear face on. It was to welcome in the parts of me I had rejected or managed and surrender false control. I didn't touch the draft of this book for a whole year. We entered a global pandemic. Life contracted in unprecedented ways — all my distractions were taken away. I was stripped of my identity in so many ways. I couldn't name the emotion I was experiencing as the shadow consumed me for much of the time. I sat in the fire, sometimes willingly, sometimes kicking and screaming.

And then, I recognised it. *Bereft.* A wise friend told me once that we have not done the work until we have felt this. To feel this as a mark of awakening? Not as a failure but a sign of evolution? I didn't understand him at the time because I thought I had everything about that phase of my life under control. Bereft means grief, mourning, sorrow. But also to be deprived of something. My ego was being starved of her addiction to being in control, fear of the unknown, panic at being rejected, and other ancient fears. She fought. Every addiction, negative self-belief, and limiting behaviour reared its head to be met. Eventually, I could no longer resist. It was like wrestling a demon. Until I remembered through total body, mind and soul exhaustion that there's no healing in wrestling. I had to put my head in the demon's mouth. I had to demonstrate that trust. I was brought to my knees. And it was divine. Wrestling is exhausting. The surrender is sublime.

It takes dedication. It takes devotion, and it takes a continual choice to put down our fear response, to put down our belief that we are a victim of the world we see, and to take up the mantle of our power. It may be terrifying. It might be glorious. We may have a different feeling about it every single day. It is far more congruent and therefore less stressful and anxiety-inducing to surrender to our God nature. To find ways to inhabit that even when things turn out different to our expectations. Did I hope that by leaving my husband and making the bold leap into the unknown, that that would be all that was required of me? Absolutely. When we empty our cup, when we put down our expectations, we find peace. God's peace and joy are mine, and this is the way it is meant to be. When we let go of all of our judgments of good or bad, we step out of the chaos of the dream. When I stopped fighting myself (as God), peace reigned. The dream lost a little more of its authority over me.

We cannot lose anything by awakening to the dream. If we don't awaken, we delay our deep joy, peace, and happiness, and that of everybody else. *A Course in Miracles* tells us that teaching is demonstrating. Teaching has nothing to do with our job title. To teach, to be a leader, we must embody what we want others to know. The law of vibration tells us that it is a vibrating universe we live in. Everything is but a vibration. If we truly want to alter someone else's life, we must change our own. All is one. When we meet our fear, we meet fear on behalf of those who don't even know it is an option. We are now leaders because we know what others do not yet know.

Our spiritual seeking is a privilege, and there are days where it feels like a heavy burden, but I want us not to be afraid of the discomfort. Don't be scared of getting uncomfortable. It's okay if not every day is sunshine and roses. Our spiritual awakening comes with a mighty responsibility. We do not awaken for ourselves alone. We must be willing to be the demonstration of our awakening, to shine our light so that others may find their way out from the darkness. To keep our spiritual awakening private or only utilised for personal gain is to break the universal laws. We must be unafraid to lead. We must walk in congruence. We must step out of the closet and give back because not all have the privilege. We do not awaken for ourselves alone.

Our faith has to be bigger than casual ideas that come and go. Spiritual seeking is so far beyond a lifestyle choice. It is to truly inhabit our holiness in wholeness, or whole of life. We don't keep the spiritual parts of our life to that 6 AM meditation or when we're doing yoga or when we go on retreat, but that we live our whole life from this place.

We no longer think that we can get in our car and be abusive to the person who cut us off in traffic and then be spiritual somewhere else. We must be willing to hand our entire life over to God and say,

*Use me.*

That will be the most delightful invitation for some of us, and we will go willingly in that direction. For others, this will feel like a terrifying proposition, but either way, the day will come for all of us in which we will say yes to the greater purpose and deeper meaning of our life.

The leader knows that their life is for a greater purpose than just their little patch of happiness and that their very reason for being here is to connect to that greater meaning. My invitation to all of us is to remember we are what others are seeking, and we are the antidote to the world gone mad. We do that not by judging the world or telling people what they should or shouldn't be thinking, but by demonstrating, by being that living, breathing expression of what God is, which is holy love.

We do this not by martyring ourselves or reducing ourselves to keep everybody else content and happy, but by being unafraid to go beyond everybody else's limits and expectations. We recognise where we live inside borrowed limits and put down that which no longer serves us with no fear. We know that we are serving at the highest level and in so doing — *live unafraid to be superconscious*.

There is no complication about our purpose. It is the same as every other human being on the planet. We are here to serve, but that service is holy. It doesn't matter what we choose to do with our life. The doing is not in what God is interested in. It is the state of being that we inhabit that matters. We now have all we need to choose a greater state of being. Here's to letting our lives be the fullest, most incredible expression of superconsciousness made manifest. We are the vanguard of the new paradigm.

## The vanguard's prayer

The forefront of a movement.

This is who I am—the new paradigm pack. I'm disruptive and proud of it.

I'm not receiving my intuition. I AM my intuition.

I'm not holding space. I'm creating it.

I don't want your trinkets. I'm the living oracle.

I don't have a gift. Or if I do, I'm one of 7 billion.

No one needs my book/my program/my offer. It's my medicine, and I'm sure as heaven going to take it.

God isn't gentle and loving. She's fierce and does not want my comfort but demands my evolution.

I don't need energetic protection. I need only to get over my separation mentality.

The Universe is not teaching me a lesson. I am the freaking Universe.

If I see signs everywhere, it's because I create them.

I am full of sound and fury, signifying nothing if I 'guide' others and take no responsibility for myself.

I can only ever be the Leader of myself because…

There. Is. Only. One. Of. Us. Here.

And so it is. And it is so.

# Acknowledgements

This book has been created in alchemy with the hundreds of students who have trained with the Institute for Intuitive Intelligence and willingly allowed me to guide them towards their superconsciousness. Their participation, experiences, and feedback have shaped the creation of this book. I am so grateful to all of you.

To my boys, who I have the privilege of raising in this life to be the full expression of who they are. To my mama and papa for giving me everything. And to Angelique for having the courage to bring Intuitive Intelligence Tapping into the world. To Angel, for being the first investor in the Institute and giving me the gift of living my purpose.

To my incredible business bestie, Institute CFO, inspiration, and friend, Laura Elkaslassy who sees what is possible and inspires me to go after it.

To my best friend Elissa Wilson for being my rock and the family that I got to choose. To my ex-husband, Julian, for continuing to be an incredible co-parent and friend. To Gemma Sykes for your constant support and friendship. You are a true soul sister.

To Elise Elliot for designing the most beautiful books for me. To Kia West for your dedication to these teachings and for whipping these words into shape. To Elisha Halpin for your wisdom and constant inspiration. The Institute is blessed to have you. To Jayne Vidler and Gemma Sykes who offered brilliant feedback and helped whip this book into shape. To Michelle Tolhurst, who makes running the Institute so much easier in every way.

# About Dr Ricci-Jane Adams

Hey, hey beloved, I'm Ricci-Jane. A researcher, writer and intuition geek dedicated to elevating your intuition to the level of superconsciousness. I have never doubted that I had a tremendous purpose in this life. Raised in a spiritual home, the path of awakening was always my passion, and I sensed that my work in the world would emerge from this passion even as a child. In 2014, with twenty plus years of intuition exploration under my belt, I was yearning to go even deeper. I wanted a university-style qualification that brought with it a community of like-minded, equally devoted and geeky intuitives. No matter where I looked, and boy did I look, I couldn't find it. I knew I had to make it. And that's what I did.

From Reiki, to dramatherapy, to theatre studies, to playwriting, to Transpersonal Counselling, and eventually even to completing a doctorate in magical realism at the University of Melbourne, seeking to know more, to become more, to understand more is at the very heart of me. Every path I have taken has always been informed by a desire to know my soul nature more intimately. What I came back to time and again was intuition. Of course, it was! Intuition is the language of the Cosmos. It is how we connect our human reality with our divine truth. It is everything.

As a researcher by trade, I set about learning everything I could about intuition. But so much of what I found left me wanting. Built on the trinkets and superstitions of the new age, many of the teachings were superficial or asked me to give my power to crystals or oracle cards, or worse to a psychic or healer. I knew undoubtedly this is our greatest spiritual skill, so why was it being shared in such a way? Intuition is the language of the cosmos. It is how we connect our human reality with our divine truth. It is everything.

I have spent the last 20 years on a quest to know the truth about intuition – how it works, what it is, where it emerges from, why it works, and even when it works! What I uncovered in researching and living and teaching all that I was learning is a revolutionary method to increasing our innate intuition that has never failed. It is a method of turning on our intuition to become a state of being, not something that we tune in and out of. My vision became so very clear. To train an extraordinary collective to take their intuition to the level of spiritual superpower so that they can support others to increase their connection to their own deepest states of intuition. Intuitive Intelligence® guides us home to the truth that we are unlimited. The Institute was created to show you how.

# About Superconscious Intuition the Program

YOU'VE COME A LONG WAY, AND YOU'VE MADE HUGE STRIDES WITH YOUR INTUITION DEVELOPMENT.

You're in a place where you live your intuition on the daily, your devotion is rocking and you make choices in partnership with God consciousness.

People tell you how intuitive you are. You've trained it, invested in it, nurtured it. But still…You yearn to go deeper. You can feel a greater power in you.

Does this sound familiar?

- You haven't sought the comfort/familiar zone for a long time.
- You live on the spiritual edge.
- You are all in for profound spiritual growth, and you dare to go where your intuition is leading.
- You have the humility within you to know that you can always go deeper, vaster, wider with your spiritual superpower. And you're aching for it.
- You want to embody your leadership in your relationship to intuition, not imitate.

- You crave rigour and guidance in the maturing of your Intuitive Intelligence.
- You long for a path of deep devotion that scaffolds you strongly.

You are ready for even more. You want to be the consistent demonstration of:

- Intuitive mastery
- Spiritual maturity
- Embodied intuition
- Powerhouse spiritual agency.

## PRACTICAL AND GUIDED ADVANCED INTUITION TRAINING

Across ten modules and ten evidence-based practices, you receive the tools, theory, and philosophy to exponentially increase your highest form of intelligence. The path of Superconscious Intuition is uncompromising because it will ask you to put down all perceived limitations. This program takes you most directly towards your unlimited personal power.

**Take the program to turn the knowledge in this book into wisdom. Learn more at:**

**study.instituteforintuitiveintelligence.com/superconscious-intuition**

Made in United States
Orlando, FL
26 April 2022

17204765R00145